STRONACH
The Village Strikes Back

WITH BEST WISHES

STRONACH

The Village Strikes Back

Norman Harper

Birlinn

First published in Great Britain in 2003 by
Birlinn Ltd
West Newington House
10 Newington Road
Edinburgh

www.birlinn.co.uk

ISBN 1 84158 288 3

British Library Cataloguing-in-Publication Data
A catalogue record for this book is available
on request from the British Library

Typeset by Hewer Text Ltd, Edinburgh
Printed and bound by Bell & Bain Ltd., Glasgow

In memory of Chrissabel Reid
(1923–2002)

Contents

Foreword

THE creation of Stronach was one of those accidents which happen from time to time in newspaper offices. The *Press and Journal* had run an extremely successful dialect column every Tuesday under the Donovan Smith by-line. Written by Bob Johnston, a sub-editor, cricket expert and one of the best-read men I have met, it told tales of life in an Aberdeen council estate and its many colourful characters, from Marigold Heap and Giles Pie, to Thuzie Girn and Flechie Dode. All the tales were told from the bewildered Anglo viewpoint of the fictional Donovan and his long-suffering wife.

Bob died in the mid-1980s and the paper's loss was immense. His cartooning skills were legendary. Even in the heat of a busy news night, Bob's lightning wit would conceive and dash off a pithy cartoon, usually involving one of his colleagues transplanted into a news story of the day.

So popular and admired were these cartoons that even those who were the butt of the humour prized them and took them home for safe keeping. Twenty years later, I still have two myself. One shows a man marching down the middle of the main street in a deserted village, the two poles of a huge banner, one in each hand, bearing the legend: 'MAGGIE OUT', a reference to the popularity of the Premier of the day.

Undeterred by his lack of support, or even attention, the man strides proudly on, jaw firm, convictions set. The caption reads: 'Alford's Day of Action March'.

After Bob's death, it occurred to me that although we could not replace Donovan Smith, we might be able to create something similar, but based in a village. Since the *Press and Journal* was primarily a rural paper, that seemed the most suitable.

For four months at the start of 1987, I played around with a core cast of likely characters. I'll confess now that virtually all of them were based on the village worthies that I knew as I was growing up in our corner of rural Aberdeenshire.

My favourite, Babbie Girn, was a feisty widow whose cutting humour was so entertaining that I used to visit her every Friday night for a fly cup and a news, just to hear her latest tale or Doric turn of phrase. It was she who told me that a neighbour was so sour-faced that she 'lookit like a hen layin razors'.

Anyway, with all the characters in place and the editorial green light for a debut in a newly revamped weekend section on August 1, 1987, we faced only one difficulty: our village had no name.

We couldn't base it on a real village for fear of being sued. We couldn't even have a name that sounded remotely similar, yet we needed something that sounded North-easty. I trawled through half a dozen gazetteers on the last weekend in July, the deadline ticking away, still with nothing.

On the Tuesday before launch, I was checking off the next day's *Press and Journal* birthday-club entries, by which children in the circulation area were wished Happy Birthday in print, when my co-checker and colleague Rena said: 'Here's a nine-year-old lad from Turriff called Stronach. What about that?'

And so the village was named Stronach at virtually the last minute and the first episode appeared on schedule, with minor amendments to accommodate the new name. You can still read that first episode in *Stronach: Volume One*, still available with *Volumes Two* and *Three* at all good bookshops (and probably a few awful ones).

Anyway, here's the fourth volume. It contains fifty tales from 1995 to 1999, as well as one of my favourites – which drew the greatest public response of all 811 episodes. It's Story 50: 'Dorothy at the Doctor', which appeared originally in 2003.

Enjoy your book.

Norman Harper
November, 2003

1. *Uncle Jeems's Will*

WALTER Dreep tugged at his collar and wished that he hadn't used quite so much starch. Formal occasions always brought him out in a sweat, and the collar was growing clammier by the minute.

A sharp powk in the ribs from his wife, Aggie, drew him to his senses.

'Stop that ficherin,' she muttered. 'Ye'll hae fowk thinkin ye're nervy.'

'I am nervy,' said Walter. 'Sittin here in a solicitor's office waitin for a will-readin. Could they nae pit a letter in the post? Aabody lookin at ye. Aabody kennin fit ye're gettin.'

'Think yersel lucky ye're here ata,' said Aggie. 'There wis a while that I wisna expectin nithing.'

'And ye really think yer Uncle Jeems his left ye something?'

'He'd plenty tae leave,' said Aggie. 'A villa in Barbados. An apartment in Las Vegas. A hoose and a fairm at Meikle Wartle. If he'd three hooses, ye can be sure that his bunk accoont winna hae been dry.'

'I dinna like ye lik this, Aggie. Ye're affa hard-soundin. Greedy, nearly.'

'If it's greedy ye're wintin,' Aggie said, 'jist look across the table. That's greedy.'

Walter's gaze lighted on Minerva Graip, née Roozer, who had also been invited to the reading of Uncle Jeems's will, and who seemed as nonchalant and calm as Aggie was fired up and furious that such a trallop – 'nae even a relation' – was present at all. 'I hinna seen her greetin once,' she muttered at Walter. 'Not once.'

There were ten people round the maple table in the solicitor's office. Aggie thought it rather sumptuously furnished for an Inverspaver practice, and wondered if Uncle Jeems's retainer hadn't been invested a little too handsomely in fixtures and fittings.

Aggie and Walter couldn't put names to faces, although they had a vague recollection of the dumpy little woman at the far corner being Jeems's housekeeper. They were still scanning the other figures, all studiously studying first their laps, then the walls, then their laps again, when the door from the side office opened and in walked Billy, Jeems's long-time solicitor.

He cut through the social niceties, then disposed of the legal preamble efficiently, although perhaps a little too efficiently for the dumpy housekeeper, who tapped her hearing aid once or twice, causing it to whistle and bring proceedings to a temporary halt.

'Now, ladies and gentlemen, we'll come to the important matter. How much?'

There was much coughing, tugging at collars, grasping of handbags and shuffling of buttocks.

'As you know, Jeems was not a poor man. He ran a tight and lucrative business, invested wisely in stocks and bonds and, although he spent lavishly on himself, he barely dented his assembled assets in so doing.'

Aggie could feel a flush coming on her.

'Were it possible to value the heritable assets on the same basis as all other holdings, a conservative estimate puts Jeems's worth on the day of his death at approximately sixteen million . . .'

The dumpy woman's eyes rolled back in their sockets and she slid from her seat and under the table.

'. . . sixteen million, nine hundred and forty-seven thousand pounds. Give or take a thousand pounds or two.' Billy flicked a switch on the intercom and asked his secretary to bring through a glass of cold water. 'On second thoughts,' he said, looking at the remainder of the document before him, 'make that a jug of water and a dozen glasses.'

Aggie shot a look across the table at Minerva, who sat cool and composed, as if she had just heard the reading of a shopping list. Aggie noted there was still nary a hint of grief about her. Definitely a trallop. Worse, a greedy trallop.

'Now,' continued Billy, 'we come to the specifics. As you know, Jeems had no direct line of descent. He was unmarried and, as far as we know, had no children extant. Consequently, the terms of his testament are somewhat unusual to say the least. You can imagine that a great deal of thought had been invested in attribut-

2

ing more than sixteen million pounds of property and investments.'

'Naturally,' said Minerva, 'James was always very careful about his assets. He looked after the things that mattered to him.' She turned to smile a cold smile at Aggie and Walter. 'And the people, of course.'

Aggie shot Minerva another look, wondering where the posh accent had come from, but Walter gripped her hand underneath the table and she bit her tongue.

'So, now, we'll go into the detail of the will. Would anybody like a comfort stop?'

From the way people were leaning forward over the table, it became apparent that a comfort stop was far from the thoughts of any of them.

'All right,' said Billy, as his secretary appeared with the tray and began ministering to the first casualty. 'We'll begin with the apartment in Las Vegas, valued, according to our American agents, at approximately half a million dollars.'

He looked up at Walter and Aggie.

Aggie, however, was scowling at Minerva.

'Look at her,' Aggie muttered at Walter. 'She's some deemie. There's been mair fingerprints on her backside than Lodge Walk's got in their files.'

Billy the lawyer coughed to draw the room to attention once more then turned to read Jeems's last testament. 'My villa in the Caribbean, set in six acres of prime residential ground, with a quarter mile of private beach, access to a jetty and the yacht has been probably my favourite possession these last twenty-five years. It has given me much pleasure to escape the winters at Meikle Wartle and to know that while I sat in comfort and warmth, my neighbours were looking after my farm and my business interests at home so well.

'For that reason, I am pleased to leave all my Caribbean interests to my good friends Harry and Daphne Queet. I also leave them the sum of £100,000 for air fares and sundry expenses.'

A ruddy-faced couple in their fifties to Aggie's right sat gasping for air. 'I dinna believe it,' said the woman. 'He aye telt us he wis in a chalet at Butlin's.'

The lawyer continued. 'To my housekeeper, Mary, who looked after me so well with her home cooking and conversation, I leave the farmhouse at Meikle Wartle and an allowance of £20,000 per year for life, so that she may live in the comfort which she always strove to bring to others.'

The little fat woman who had fainted earlier began sobbing gently into her hankie, and the others looked away in mild embarrassment.

'To my nephew, Bertram, who maintained always that I should be a little more enterprising than just farming tatties at Wartle, I wish I could see your face now you impudent vratch but, seeing as he is my only flesh and blood, I leave him the farm, exclusive of the farmhouse, and hope that he will hold back on some of his dafter ideas and try to follow the business plan my advisers and I have set out in separate documentation.'

A man in his early forties in an ill-fitting Sunday-best suit tugged at his collar and flushed beetroot-red. A mousy little woman sitting next to him powked him sharply in the ribs.

'To Wullie and Elsie Hoast, who have done such sterling work for our Highland Games committee, I leave a lump sum of £80,000, on condition that it be used to renovate existing premises or to find new ones, and to ensure that the games are the best of their kind in Northeast Scotland.'

A couple in their late sixties nodded, almost as if they had been expecting it.

'Which brings me to the apartment in Las Vegas and my stocks and bonds which, at current values, stand at roughly £4.6 million.

Aggie could feel herself sweating profusely and she managed to steal a glance across at Minerva, who remained ice-cool.

'Now I come to my grand-niece by marriage, Agnes, and her husband, Walter, whom I have not seen for almost twenty years. I might have lived at the other side of Mars for all the effort they put into visiting me. It caused me a great deal of sorrow to know that they valued my company so poorly, and that I have not seen hide nor hair of their son, Samuel.

'Consequently, I leave them nothing.'

There was a shuffle of embarrassment. Aggie was too stunned to react and she stared into her lap, while Walter smiled a weary little smile to himself. Easy come, easy go.

Minerva, meanwhile, had done all the mental calculations and had sat up in her seat, smoothing down her skirt.

'Which brings me finally to Minerva Roozer, who went to quite the other extreme and visited me almost every other evening in the mid-1960s.'

Minerva smiled and leaned forward.

'She was usually in short skirts, painted to the nines and stinking of cheap scent. Minerva, I don't know what you thought you were doing all those years, but I was never so glad as the day you lost interest and stormed off to Banffshire to inflict your cheap vulgarity on some poor unfortunate fisherman.

'I could not rest easy knowing that a cheap trallop had her grasping hands on almost five million pounds of mine. Accordingly, you get nothing but my pity for your transparent greed. The remainder of my estate will be put into a foundation which my lawyers will establish for the furtherance of the Doric. Five million should be a good start for something that is long overdue.'

THEY walked into the sun a few minutes later, several of them substantially richer and beaming smiles which said so.

'Ye're nae fashin, are ye?' said Walter, taking Aggie's elbow.

'Nivver a fash,' said Aggie. 'Fit he said wis quite richt. We didna visit aften. It's wir ain lookoot.'

'Nivver mind,' said Walter, 'ye got yer wish anither wye.' He nodded across to the other side of the car park.

There stood Minerva Graip, gripping the railings, face buried in a hankie, howling and sobbing with rage.

'Ye see,' said Walter, 'she can greet efter aa.'

2 Two Nights on the Tiles

FLO Spurtle was stirring the pan of bolognaise sauce, but Gibby thought that she was stirring it a little more animatedly than usual. He wondered if he had made a mistake in being honest.

'And ye're sure this is absolutely essential?' said Flo without looking round. 'I mean, it's nae as if this wifie's a relation or nithing.'

'She's been a Crochlie Neuk resident since ivver the place opened,' said Gibby. 'And now she's turnin a hunder. She's haein a little party for aa her chums and I'm invited. It wid look a bittie aff if I wisna there. I mean, fit wid be said? There'll be a telegram fae the Queen, a photiegrapher fae the *Press and Journal*, bit the gairdener couldna bother tae turn up.'

'You attend this party if ye like, Gibby,' said Flo. 'It's nae concern o mine. Aa that I'm sayin is if you come hame drunk or wi yer best claes torn, and us supposed tae be gaun for my birthday denner in the Toon the morn's nicht, ye'll ken o't.'

Gibby planted a wet kiss on his wife's cheek. 'I kent fine ye'd see sense, petal.'

THE party was well under way by the time Gibby arrived. The residents were decked out in their finery, sporting foil hats and blowing tooteroos. The photographer had been and gone.

'He wis a bittie rushed,' one of the other residents told Gibby. 'Something aboot an affa talented hen at Abyne.'

Gibby strode across to where the birthday girl sat holding court. He waited patiently for a few moments until he caught her eye, whereupon her face lit up and she flung open her arms. 'Gilbert,' she said. 'Come intae ma bosie.' And Gibby, a little sheepishly it must be said, advanced and stooped to receive the embrace.

'Hiv ye met ma grand-dother, Louise?' she said, beaming, and nodding behind Gibby.

He spun round.

There stood someone in her late twenties, or perhaps early thirties, who looked as if she had stepped off the cover of a clubbie book. She smiled coyly and held out her hand.

'Pleased tae meet ye,' said Gibby.

'I've heard such a lot about you,' said Louise. Her voice had that husky quality that made Gibby's knees wobble. 'Great-grandma says you're quite a performer in the potting shed,' she said. 'Such a pity it's dark. I could do with a few tips.'

Gibby could feel a heat building under his collar. 'Aye, weel,' he said. 'I've finished ma wark for the day. We're here tae enjoy wirsels.'

'Dry Martini and lemonade.'

'I beg yer pardon?'

'I'd like a dry Martini and lemonade. The bar's that way.' She put one hand on his shoulder and turned him ever so gently towards the temporary bar.

He returned moments later with her drink and was surprised to see her down it in two gulps. 'It's such a refreshing drink, don't you think?'

Gibby looked at his tomato juice.

'Shall I get you one?' said Louise. 'I'm sure you'd like it.' Without waiting for an answer she glided across to the bar for a recharge. Gibby could help but notice the slinky walk; a marvel considering the height of her blue stilettos.

She returned with two drinks and offered him one. 'Thank ye, bit no,' he said. 'I'm on the tomata juice the nicht. I've anither function the morn's nicht and I need a clear heid.'

Louise ran a finger down his lapel. 'Such a popular boy,' she breathed. 'What do you have that other men don't?' Gibby shuffled awkwardly.

She swigged one Martini and lemonade and took a sip of the second.

'Ye fairly like yer Martinis,' observed Gibby.

'I find it gives me . . .' she ran her hand down his lapel again, then looked deep into his eyes '. . . ideas.' And she smiled.

'I've an idea I'm hungry,' said Gibby. 'I see there's a boofie ower in the corner. Excuse me.'

'Oh, but I'm quite peckish myself,' said Louise, grasping his elbow. 'I feel like something meaty.'

As they strode towards the buffet, Louise swigged the last of her third Martini and put the glass on a shelf.

She was to have seven more in the next hour and a half.

STRONACH'S newest centenarian had rarely looked more upset. 'Please, Gilbert,' she said. 'I dinna ken fit else tae dee. I didna think she wid get this bad. I'm black-affrontit, I dinna mind admittin. I'll pey yer petrol.'

Gibby looked at Louise slumped at the end of the settee. What had once been so elegant now looked pathetic in drink.

'Jist drive her hame. Please. I widna ask onybody bit you, because I ken ye're a decent loon. Onywye, aabody else here's been drinkin.'

Visions of Flo crowded Gibby's head, then he looked once more at the snoring form of Louise.

'Aaricht,' he said. 'Bit if Flo gets tae hear aboot this, I'll expect you tae back me up.'

'I'll phone her now,' said the old lady.

'No!' Gibby stepped towards her, then backed off. 'I mean, dinna dee that jist yet.'

It took Gibby several minutes to get the unconscious young woman into the passenger seat of his car, and then belted in. She stayed that way for more than half the journey. But gradually, as the drink began to wear off, she began giggling. Then she slipped off her shoes.

'Hello, you big animal man, you,' she said. 'Where are we going?'

'I'm takkin ye hame. Yer grandmither's affa upset wi ye.'

'She's too sensitive,' said Louise. She fumbled with the top buttons of her blouse.

'Dinna dee that!' said Gibby. A car coming towards them tooted its horn and Gibby swerved back to his own side of the road. 'Dinna dee that. I canna tak ye hame half-naked.'

'You're so shy for a big boy.' She hitched her skirt up above her knee, and Gibby sensed in the dark that her hand was wandering towards his thigh.

'Stop that,' he said. 'I'm nae haein nae capers in this car.'

Once he had decanted Louise, Gibby broke the speed limit almost all the way back to Stronach, lest Flo get suspicious. He parked on the street, rather than at the back of the house, and left the doors open for fully five minutes to try to get rid of any last lingering perfume in the car.

Flo was already in bed, but was sitting up reading. She looked up as he came in.

'Well?' she said. 'Are ye aa in ae bit?'

'A rare nicht,' he said, lying mercilessly.

'Ye seem sober enough. Ye're aa set for the morn's nicht?'

'I deliberately stuck tae tomata juice aa nicht so I wid enjoy masel wi you on yer birthday,' he said.

Flo began sniffing. 'Perfume?' she said.

A heat flashed through Gibby. 'Oh, it's the aul wifie,' he said. 'She got that mony perfumes for presents that she tried them aa on at the same time. It wis like haein a party in a chemist's.'

'Well, hing up yer claes and come in here aside me. Ye need a gweed nicht's sleep. There's nithing gaun tae spile ma big nicht the morn.'

GIBBY stood by the passenger door as Flo walked down the garden path in her finery. He had to admit that he had married a striking woman. Her cleaners' overalls didn't do her justice. With time and effort, she could look as stunning as any supermodel.

He opened the car door. 'Yer carriage, madame,' he said.

'Thank ye, Jeeves. Haud gyaun and dinna spare the cuddies.'

They were half-way to Aberdeen, and the conversation was bright and lively, when Flo dropped an ear-ring down the side of her seat. She fumbled for a moment or two, then Gibby said: 'See, I'll get it.' With an eye on the road, he fumbled under her seat.

'Oh, michty,' he said.

'Fit's adee?'

'Eh? Oh, nithing. He pulled out the ear-ring and presented it to Flo, but the conversation evaporated from that point on. Gibby had found a blue stiletto under the seat.

He was just reaching the last approaches into Aberdeen when he had an idea. He opened the window. 'Fresh air,' he explained to Flo.

A few hundred yards farther on, he pointed across to his left. 'Wid ye look at that hooses?' he said. 'Fa wid bide in monstrosities like that? And fowk shouldna parade aboot in their bedrooms wi nithing on.'

As Flo strained for a look, Gibby whipped the stiletto from under the side of her seat and flung it out the window.

Fifteen minutes later, they were drawing up outside the restaurant. Gibby switched off the engine.

9

'Gibby,' said Flo. 'Jist ae thing afore we ging in.' She leaned across and kissed his nose. 'I ken this nicht's jist gaun tae be perfect.'

Gibby smiled, then opened his door. When he reached Flo's door and opened it, he found his wife fumbling in the footwell. She looked up.

'I say, Gibby,' she said. 'Ye hinna seen ma ither shoe, hiv ye?'

3 Supermarket Calamity

THE kitchen at the Brose household was unusually haphazard for once. The array of bowls, tins, trays, packets and jars suggested that Geneva was in the midst of a larger batch of cooking than usual.

She had agreed to cook an evening meal for Sandy's brother and his wife. An early Easter holiday had brought them north from exile in Shropshire, and Sandy, as was the way with many husbands, had insisted that they visit for a meal one evening as 'Geneva steers up a rare pot o broth.'

Only Geneva's timely arrival by the phone had prevented him inviting them to stay in the spare room. As it was, evening meal was bad enough.

She had explained that while Sandy's brother might have been a homely, couthie sort, his wife was anything but: a harridan of that type peculiar to the North-east who imagines that a promotion for her husband sets her apart, and who begins clipping her vowels and shopping at Sainsbury's.

'I jist dee plain country cookin,' Geneva had told her husband at call's end. 'If it disna hae saaces and decorations ower the heid o aathing, that wifie'll turn up her nose. I ken fine.'

Sandy had waved away her protests and had turned to read his paper, which had only made matters worse.

In the five days that followed, Geneva had threatened several times to book herself into a B&B somewhere and leave Sandy to get on with the entertaining, but Sandy had pointed out each time that he would send out for white-pudding suppers to the chipper, knowing that that would call Geneva's bluff.

So Geneva had come to be wrestling with her menu and her culinary skills in her kitchen last Saturday. Her first attempt, a rolled joint later to be wrapped in pastry and presented as beef wellington, had had to be called off after the joint had shrunk so much in cooking that it would barely have fed a poodle, let alone five hearty humans, so Geneva had decided to fall back on her standard chicken supremes.

She had rummaged about in the freezer for several minutes before finding the tub marked 'chicken breasts' and had prised open the lid to find not four hearty chicken fillets but two of the saddest and weediest-looking chicken breasts it had been her misfortune to encounter. She checked the inventory she kept glued to the side of the freezer and noted that four chicken breasts were billed as being inside.

With the heat of anger and the foretaste of gross embarrassment rising in her, she realised that the meal Sandy had cooked for her birthday night several weeks before had cost her two of the fillets she had been expecting to cook.

She looked at the clock, then began rummaging in the rest of the freezer. She emerged a minute later knowing that unless she had a recipe which involved peas, freezer jam and fish fingers, she would be shamed in less than four hours.

She looked through the side window. Sandy had left the car. She reached for her purse. She could be down to the supermarket at Inverspaver and back within an hour. She paused by the mirror at the door. Rollers were hardly the headgear of choice on a shopping expedition. She raked through a drawer and found a headsquare.

CALAMITY. The freezer at the supermarket at Inverspaver was devoid of decent sized chicken fillets. There were a couple of tiny things in blue-polystyrene trays, but nothing of an order that would feed five. She stopped a white-coated assistant wheeling a rack of dairy goods and explained her plight.

'I'm affa sorry,' said the man. 'I dinna think there's onything else.'
Geneva wailed. 'That little things there widna feed a rat,' she told him. 'I need them a lot bigger than that. Hiv ye nithing ata?'

The man looked at his watch.

'Hing on a mintie,' he said. 'There wis a delivery due twinty minutes ago. If ye can wait here, I'll hae a rake ben the back and see if there's something that wid suit. I canna promise and, even if there is something, I canna pit them oot on the shelves yet until the boss signs them through, so we'll hae tae be canny.'

'It disna maitter,' said Geneva. 'As lang's ye're quick. I hinna muckle time and I'm stannin here dressed like a bloomin target. I dinna ken fit I'll say if I see onybody I ken. This is affa embarrassin.'

'I'll be as quick's I can,' said the assistant. 'We winna embarrass ye.' He abandoned his rack and trotted off behind the scenes.

Geneva slunk into a corner between processed fish and vegetarian ready meals. She tried turning her back to the the other shoppers at first, but then turned round again when she realised that some of the other staff were looking at her suspiciously.

At one stage, she spotted a couple of Stronach farmers' wives and tugged her headsquare as far down over her forehead as she could get it, then stooped to pretend she was studying the price of vegetarian sausages intently.

She was just on the point of turning round again, confident that her two acquaintances had passed, when she spied a couple from the community council. Geneva whipped round again. Two minutes later, it was the Macfarlane family from the new house at the top end of Stronach. Geneva was breaking out in a light sheen with all the strain of staying incognita.

Relieved that she had survived three narrow squeaks and that her dignity was intact, she peered towards the service door, hoping for sign of the assistant.

That was when the public-address system buzzed.

BING-BONG!

'Wid Mrs Geneva Brose from Stronach, the lady who wants bigger breasts, please meet George at the back door?'

4 A Tootle in the Country

VIRGINIA Huffie was standing by her net curtains, waiting for her lift, when she saw the Mini round the bend at the foot of the street and crawl slowly towards her. She waited for a few seconds more, just to be sure that it was the right car.

When she heard the faint tooting and saw the lights flash once or twice, Virginia scooped up her handbag and her coat and headed for the front door.

A couple of minutes later, she was in the back seat and off for a Sunday run with Euphemia Pink, the village teacher, and Miss Pink's spinster sister, Tibby.

'Isn't it an affa bonnie day for March?' said Virginia, settling herself into the tight space.

'We hidna a day as bonnie as this aa last summer,' said Tibby, smiling at the countryside they were bowling through.

'And it's real nice o ye tae think o takkin me oot on yer runnie,' said Virginia. 'Tae tell ye the truth, I'm a bittie lost athoot Babbie, although I'd nivver let on til her face.'

'She's away at Fraserburgh seeing relatives, isn't she?' said Miss Pink.

'Jist for a twa–three days,' said Virginia.

'Well, we're very happy to get you out and about, dear,' said Miss Pink. 'It makes a change for us to have company, too.'

She crunched a gear and Virginia grimaced. 'Are we gaun onywye in particular?' asked Virginia.

'Well, we like to travel the back roads,' said Miss Pink. 'That way, we avoid all the speeding traffic and you see parts of the countryside that people never see because they're always in such a hurry with themselves to get somewhere else.

'Also, we've got a wee picnic in the boot, and we've learned through experience that the best places for picnics are the edges of little woods off the back roads, rather than those formally laid-out lay-by things on the busy ones. Isn't that right, Elizabeth?'

'Couldna agree mair, Euphemia.'

'And div ye go shoppin?' asked Virginia.

'Sometimes, we do. And sometimes we go in for afternoon tea to a little tearoom somewhere, although I'm not sure if the season will be started so early. Anyway, we always find it very entertaining because we know so many people.'

'How's that?'

'Wi Euphemia bein a teacher,' said Tibby, 'ye'd be amazed foo mony o her former pupils turn up aa ower the place. There's times I think she's educatit a squad o waitresses. There's whiles I think there's hardly a caffy in the hale o the North-east that hisna got een o Euphemia's lassies in it.'

'Is that so?' said Virginia.

Miss Pink wheeled off the main highway suddenly and on to the hill road. A BMW driver coming towards them braked violently and flashed his lights. Tibby gave him a cheery wave. 'Affa friendly fowk hereaboots,' she observed.

Once Virginia's palpitations had settled, she asked again about the ubiquity of Miss Pink's former pupils.

'Oh, well,' said Miss Pink. 'I think Sister gilds the lily just a little, but it's true that we have chanced upon former Stronach boys and girls in all sorts of odd corners.' A rabbit scuttled across the road and Miss Pink braked so hard that Virginia's handbag flew through to the front of the car.

'She's a member o the National Trust,' said Tibby, as if that explained it.

The trio travelled for fully two hours, admiring castle ruins, budding trees, work in the fields and the number of new houses being erected in odd rural corners. They were just rounding a bend near Huntly when the sight of orange flashing lights made Miss Pink slam on the anchors for the seventeenth time that morning and, once again, Virginia's handbag took off round the car cabin.

The two Misses Pink peered in front at the tractor, its trailer and a large pile of dung. A strapping young lad in his late twenties seemed to be forking over the dung, but as the trailer was protruding into the road there seemed little chance of progress.

'Awa oot and hae words wi him, Euphemia,' advised Tibby. 'Pit on yer teacher face. Scare him.'

'He's only doing his job,' said Miss Pink. 'This is farmland, after all.'

'It's a public road,' said Tibby. 'If you dinna ging oot, I'll ging oot.'

'Shall we all three of us go out?' said Miss Pink. 'It's a lovely day for a walk.'

As soon as they opened the car doors, the smell of ripe manure clothed them like a treacle bath.

'That fairly clears the tubes,' said Tibby, taking a deep breath, then coughing. 'There's fowk pays money for that in Aiberdeen.'

The trio strode towards the tractor. The farmhand carried on dellin the dung. Only when he caught sight of them did he stop for a moment, and the three Stronach woman could see that his shirt was soaked through and rivers of sweat were running down his face and his bare arms.

'Ladies,' he said, but he carried on working.

'Are you likely to be much longer?' said Miss Pink tentatively.

The young man looked at the large pile of dung on the road. 'A whilie yet, I doot,' he said. 'Affa sorry, bit it aa fell aff the back as I wis turnin in through the gate.' Then, for the first time, he stopped.

'Miss Pink?' he said.

Miss Pink looked more closely at him. 'David? David Scurl?'

'It's been a lang time,' he said. 'Nineteen sivventy-five I wis in your class at Stronach Primary.'

'David, how nice to catch up with you. And you're doing fine? Your career's going well?'

David looked round at the monstrous heap of manure. 'Apart fae shovellin dung in an affa day o heat, ye mean?'

Miss Pink thought for a moment. 'Listen,' she said, half-turning as if to go back to the car. 'We've a lovely picnic in the back of the car. There's no traffic at all. It won't matter if you take a half-hour longer or so. And I'm sure we've got enough for four. Why don't you stop and have a bite to eat with us?'

'Thank ye, Miss Pink, bit I couldna even think o't. The fairmer'll be needin this back in the cairt real quick.' He began digging and throwing again.

'You can surely spare just twenty minutes,'

'Na, fegs. The fairmer wid flail me alive. This is a real rush job.'

'I can't believe that such abuse of staff exists in this day and age.

He should be ashamed of himself, working his staff to a greasy spot.'

'Weel, if ye canna jine wir picnic, fit aboot a drink, than?' said Tibby, smiling up at him. 'Ye can surely tak a mintie for a drink. I can see jist fae the look o ye that ye need a lang, caul drink. Ye've a face like a turkey cock.'

Still, digging, Davie licked his lips, but shook his head. 'Nae even a minute,' he said. 'I canna. Ye dinna ken this fairmer. It wid be mair than ma life's worth.'

'Are you serious, David?' said Miss Pink.

'I'm perfectly serious,' said David, still digging. 'He's a real hard taskmaster. I'd better hurry.'

'Even in hot weather like this?'

'Especially in hot weather lik this.'

Miss Pink thought for a moment, then her teacher face stole upon her and, jaw set firm, she stepped gingerly towards her former pupil.

'What's the name of this farmer? And where does he live? I think I need to have a few words with this man. Nobody abuses one of my former pupils without having me to answer to.'

'Honestly, Miss Pink, I wid raither ye didna. Jist let me get on wi ma work. I hinna time for argyin.'

'I insist, David. Where can I find this man?'

David sighed, but carried on digging.

'Ye'll get him in anither twa minutes,' he said. 'As seen as I get him oot fae aneth this load o dung.'

5 Sammy's Career Move

AGGIE Dreep stood at the bottom of the stairs. 'Sammy,' she called. 'Bus in 10 minutes. Get up and get oot or ye'll miss it.'

She returned to the kitchen, where her husband, Walter, was devouring a slice of dry wholemeal toast while he scanned his *Press and Journal.* 'An affa deaths the day,' he observed. 'Here's een. 'Suddenly at the Boogaloo Disco Club, Kintore. Mirabelle Duncan, aged 92. Dearly loved mother, grandmother and Garioch senior disco champion.'

'If yer loon disna get up in the next twa minutes, his boss'll kill him and he'll be appearin in the deaths the morn,' Aggie said.

'He's nivver usually this late,' Walter said. He looked at his watch, then at the clock on the wall. 'He's been gettin slower and slower this past whilie. Since he got passed up for that promotion, he's hid a face like a weet nicht lookin for a dry mornin.'

Aggie put her mug of coffee on the table and sat down. 'Weel,' she said, 'it must be affa disappintin, workin awa at yer job and gettin naewye, fin aa yer colleagues is gettin promotit at the drap o a hat.'

'Five minutes,' Walter said. 'That's aa he's got noo. He'll nae hae time for brakfist. Ye'd better mak up something in a plastic box for him. Sandwiches and an aipple or something. I'll awa and raise him.'

Moments later, Walter returned. 'I've cried and cried at him, bit nae response.'

Walter returned to the living-room. As he reached the bottom of the stairs, a shadow fell across the lobby and the windows rattled as the Aberdeen bus bowled past. That was one deadline beyond concern.

He climbed the staircase, tapped quietly on his son's bedroom door then grasped the handle and poked his head round the corner. Sammy was sitting upright in bed, head flopped to one side, gazing in the general direction of the dressing-table.

'Ye've missed yer bus,' Walter said.

Sammy didn't look round. 'It's nae my bus noo,' he said.

Walter stepped inside and sat down on the end of the bed.

'Nae your bus noo?'

'It's nae my job noo, eether' Sammy said. 'I packed it in on Friday. I spent five year in that mailroom and nivver got onywye. The boy that startit the same time as me's jist been made managin director. Am I supposed tae be happy aboot that?'

'Bit he wis the boss's son,' Walter said. 'Ye've tae expect favouritism like that. That's nae reflection on your skills. I bet they werena pleased at ye jackin in yer job efter five year.'

'They couldna hiv cared less. The service manager said I could please masel because he'd twinty fowk on a waitin list for my job. Nae even a cheerio. There ye are, dad. That's the wye o the corporate world nooadays. Ye're nae a person. Ye're jist a number.'

'And now that ye've tae start fae scratch,' Walter said, 'see this nae as a setback, bit as an opportunity.'

'Fit div ye mean?'

'Aa that book-learnin ye've got. Ye've letters efter yer name. Ye've an education. Ye've a degree. They coont for something.'

'Nae muckle,' Sammy said. 'In my time, we thocht a degree wis essential. Now graduates is startin careers wi three years' less experience o a job than school-leavers hiv.'

'Bit somebody needs an expert in . . . fit's yer degree again?'

'Criminal psychology and industrial pyrotechnology.'

'There ye go. There must be dizzens o companies in Scotland needin a consultant in fibs and squibs.'

'Dinna think so,' Sammy said. 'I've got the degree, bit I hinna the practical experience. Jist face the fact that I wastit ma time at the university and I'm wastin ma time noo. I'd hiv been better aff leavin the school at sixteen.'

'That's nae true.'

'Of coorse it's true. I'm twinty-five and I'm deein the kinna jobs that lads o sixteen dee.'

'Ye hinna a job ata noo.'

'I'll get a job this aifterneen. I've an interview at Inverspaver.'

'Fit for?'

'Deputy adipose culinary practitioner.'

'Oh, yer mither'll be pleased. Fit's that? A health inspector for the cooncil?'

'Apprentice frier at the Inverspaver chipper.'

Walter's shoulders sank. 'Ye're underplayin yersel again, loon,' he said. 'Ye've sae muckle talent. Sae muckle intelligence. Ye jist dinna believe in yer ain abilities. Ye could be somebody instead o stannin at a frier nicht efter nicht sheilin chips and comin hame stinkin o vinegar and fat.'

'Better than bein unemployed,' Sammy said. 'And it's a trainin.'

'A trainin?' Walter said. 'Fit trainin div ye need tae fry chips?'

'Ye'd be surprised,' Sammy said. 'There's mair tae rinnin a chipper than fowk think. It's nae jist stannin there in a white coat and a stupid hat, fryin chips, blaain yer nose and tellin drunks tae behave themsels. There's a lot mair on a chipper menu nooadays than jist chips and huggis suppers. There's mair than a hunner different hings that I've tae learn foo tae cook.'

'Such as?'

'Pineapple fritters. Aipple fritters. Mars Bar fritters. Ice cream fritters.'

'Exactly,' Walter said. 'That sums ye up. Ye're fritterin yer life awa.'

6 *Gibby's Chat-up Lines*

GIBBY Spurtle fumbled in his pocket for change as he approached the little shed. It was not a particularly salubrious shed, but it did sterling service as an admissions booth at the main gate of the showpark whenever the vale held some sort of community event.

'Hello, Babbie,' he said, peering towards the showring. 'Ye've got a fair steer. The hale village b'the look o't.'

'Three poun, please,' said Babbie. 'No, there's hardly onybody fae the village, and I'm real annoyed aboot it. They couldna haul themsels awa fae their TVs for ae Sunday aifterneen. Maist o the fowk in there's strangers. Toonsers, by the spik o them.'

'Nae locals ata?'

'Sammy Dreep's aboot the stretch o't. Sammy's got a face lik a weet nicht lookin for a dry mornin. Lord knows fit wye he bathered comin oot if he's that depressed. A puckle aul tractors at a vintage-tractor show widna raise onybody's spirits. Dinna quote me. Onywye, ye're haudin up the queue. Awa wi ye.'

Gibby took his ticket and stepped away from the admissions gate. He stood for a few seconds to get his bearings, then strode towards the refreshments tent.

He ducked down as he entered the small marquee and picked his way across the grass to the trestle table where Walter Dreep was doing duty.

'A halfie tae be gaun on wi, Wattie, if ye please,' he said.

Walter pulled the ring on a can of lager, topped it with an upturned plastic cup and shoved it towards Gibby.

'I'm richt pleased ye're here,' he whispered. He fumbled in his own pocket for three pound coins and dropped them into the cashbox. 'This drink's on me if ye'll dee me a big favour.'

'If I can.'

'Look ower in the corner.'

Gibby turned round to see Sammy, Walter's son, sitting disconsolately at a table for eight. The fact that he was on his own at such a large table heightened the pathos.

'He's been affa depressed lately,' said Walter. 'We dinna ken if it's money or the college or whether him and Floretta hiv splutten up. We ken he thinks a lot o you, Gibby. Can you get it oot o him and see if ye can pit him richt?'

SAMMY scarcely looked up when Gibby sat down beside him. 'Anither orange juice, Sammy?'

Sammy looked up and smiled a smile so thin that it barely registered. 'No, thanks,' he said 'I'm fine.'

Gibby looked at the empty plastic cup in front of his companion, then at the tired features on the young man himself. 'Ye dinna look fine tae me,' he said. 'Something adee?'

'Me and Floretta's split up.'

'Again?'

'For good this time. She wis affa nice aboot it, bit she said she couldna tie hersel doon wi a permanent student. She said some fowk wis already millionaires by the time they reached my age. She said I'd lost the ambition and the enthusiasm that attracted her in the first place. She said I hidna ma charm nae mair. She said she wis affa sorry, but she thocht I'd be better aff athoot her.'

His head dropped forward as he finished, and Gibby supposed that he might have been hiding a moistness about the eyes.

'Bit ye're absolutely stinkin wi charm,' said Gibby.

'Ye're makkin a feel o me noo, Gibby,' said Sammy. 'I ken I'm nae Romeo. I ken I'm nae affa ambitious. I ken I hinna got the patter. Nae like you.'

Gibby felt the enjoyable glow of flattery. 'Weel, I hiv been telt that I've got a wye wi the fillies, richt enough.'

'Learn me.'

'Learn ye fit?'

'A wye wi the ladies. Learn me.'

'I canna learn ye something lik that,' said Gibby. 'Ye've either got it or ye hinna. It's a natural talent. Ye canna learn it oot o books or get it in a classroom. It's jist yer wye.'

'Show me your wye.' Sammy nodded behind Gibby, who turned

round to see two young women in jeans and T-shirts sitting down with cans of cola two tables away.

Gibby turned back. 'Are ye aff yer heid, min? I'm mairriet. If news o a chat-up got back tae Flo, I'd be oot. Ma feet widna touch.'

'Then tell me fit tae say.'

Gibby studied him for a moment. There was glint of determination about him.

'Jist a coupla lines,' said Sammy. He was pressing now.

'OK,' said Gibby. He leaned forward and lowered his voice to a whisper. 'Ging across and ask them if they'd like a drink.'

'Bit they've got drinks.'

'That's nae the pint. Ye've broken the ice. They lach and you apologise for yer mistake and ye sit doon wi them. Ye ask them fit's taen bonnie young lassies lik them for a day oot amon aul tractors and then – whoosh – ye're aff lik a bleezin lum.'

'Ye're sure?'

'Tried and tested by the master. Ye canna fail.'

Sammy took a deep breath, grasped the edge of the table for a second or two, then said: 'All systems go' and pushed himself to his feet.

Gibby gave him an encouraging smile and a nod in the girls' direction. As Sammy left, Gibby half-turned his chair so that he could survey his pupil's progress.

He watched as Sammy stopped by the girls' table and they looked up. He could not hear the conversation, but he saw them speaking to Sammy, then saw Sammy's shoulders slump. A moment later, Sammy had turned and was shuffling back towards him.

'Weel?' said Gibby.

Sammy flopped back into his seat.

'I askit them if they'd like a drink. They said they'd already got drinks. Wis I blin, as stupid as I lookit or jist somebody fae the country?'

'So you said?'

'I said nithing ata,' wailed Sammy. 'Ye're best nae argyin if ye get the dunt lik that.'

'Bit they wis jist testin ye,' said Gibby. 'It's a pairt o the game o love. If they're chikky tae you, they're really needin you tae be a bittie chikky back. Banter braks the ice. The three o ye ends up lachin and – whoosh – ye're aff like a bleezin lum.'

'I canna tak nae mair o this bleezin lum,' said Sammy. 'You show me.'

'OK,' he said. 'Stand weel back. Listen, learn and admire an expert.'

He strode across to the girls' table; smiled what he imagined was his most alluring smile, and said: 'Hullo, angels. Hiv ye jist drappit in fae Heaven specially for yours truly?'

The two girls studied him. 'The only thing that's drappit here,' said the blonde, 'is your belly ower the tap o yer troosers.'

Gibby was thrown for a moment. 'Very good. Very good,' he conceded. 'So wid ye like tae come roon and see the show wi's?'

'Wid you lik tae tak yer ugly face back far it come fae?' said the blonde.

Gibby turned round and winked at Sammy. Time for the killer punch.

'Sorry,' said Gibby. 'I made a mistake. I thocht ye wis ma mither and ma untie. It must be yer make-up and yer claes.'

He turned, winked again at Sammy, and began to walk away.

'I canna be yer mither,' shouted the blonde.

Gibby stopped and smiled, then turned round slowly.

'And fit wye's that, darlin?'

'Because I'm mairriet.'

7 Erchie Claims the Glory

THE bustle at the Stronach Arms was almost predictable. John the Barman was rushed off his feet with trade of Hogmanay proportions – and all thanks to a tale of pensioner heroism that had the entire nation agog.

The many TV crews and reporters had returned Down South, but the throng of regulars around the bar remained enthralled and was studying the double-page spread in that morning's *Press and Journal*:

Stronach widow disarms knife-wielding murder maniac with chocolate sponge
Secret-recipe cake tames multiple-slash fiend.

'THEY fairly build up yer excitement at the daily paper,' observed Sandy Brose, as he scanned the library pictures of seven-times knife-murderer Slasher McGurk, the man who had kept Sammy and Aggie Dreep hostage in their own home until Babbie Girn had arrived with a fly cup on a tray and had demanded his knife to cut her chocolate sponge.

'She'll likely get a medal, Babbie will,' suggested Fobbie Pluffer. 'That must hiv taen nerves o steel. Nerves o steel, it must hiv taen.'

'Did I ivver tell ye,' said Erchie Sotter from the side of the crowd, 'aboot the time I . . .'

'I can jist see her noo,' continued Fobbie, 'doon at Buckingham Palace in front o the Queen, for a commendation and a gong peened til her breist.'

'There'll likely be a ceevic reception at Inverspaver cooncil chamber,' said Gibby Spurtle. 'Babbie'll be the guest o honour.'

'It wis like the time,' said Erchie, pressing on gamely, 'that I wis up til ma oxters in . . .'

'I widna be surprised supposin she gets a parchment fae the chief constable,' said Sandy Brose. 'He's aye handin oot bravery parchments. And ye canna say she wisna brave.'

'As brave as the time,' said Erchie, 'that I saved a mannie fae certain death and . . .'

'And she's a pensioner, that's the thing that gets me,' said John the Barman. 'It proves that ye're nivver ower aul ti hae backbone and dee yer bit.'

'Spikkin aboot deein yer bit . . .'

'There's folk half her age widna hiv dared try that,' said Sandy. 'And now she's putten Stronach on the map, fair and square. I canna hardly believe it.'

'LIKE THE TIME I PUT STRONACH ON THE MAP MASEL!' shouted Erchie.

A silence fell over the bar and they turned to look at their compatriot. Erchie looked almost surprised by the effect, tugged at the neck of his sark as if to say: 'That's mair like the thing' and took a sip of his beer.

'I ken we'll regret this, boys,' said John, 'bit, OK, Erchie, foo did you pit Stronach on the map?'

'I stoppit a boy deein awa wi himsel.'

'Oh, aye, and fit wye wis he deein awa wi himsel?'

'Because,' said Erchie, 'like a lot o us fa's talents is kept under a tree, he felt the hale world wis against him. He thocht the hale world didna recognise his skills.'

'Fa's this like?' said Sandy.

'Ye winna hae heard o him. He wis a fairmer's loon fae Abyne wye that wis wi me in the desert during the war. That young loon did mair tae keep wir spirits up than the hale o ENSA combined. He wrote richt bonnie sangs. He wrote sangs aboot Deeside and Buchan and the rollin hills o the Cabrach, and he hid aa o's near greetin wi hamesickness ilky nicht, he wis that good.'

'So if he wis that good, fit wye hiv we nae heard o him?' inquired Gibby.

'Exackly,' said Erchie. 'Ma pint, exackly. Fan we wis demobbed, he took up sangwritin full time fae the fairmhoose near Abyne. He sent them til aa the music companies and he jist got them sent back wi real chikky letters.'

'He couldna hiv been affa good, than,' said John.

'It wisna that ava,' said Erchie. 'Appeerently, the music companies said his sangs wis ower similar til stuff that wis already on the market.'

'Such as?'

'Well, he wis the boy that wrote "The Yellow Rose of Kemnay".'

The regulars looked at each other blankly.

'And he wisna a success wi that?' asked John.

'Not a myowt,' said Erchie. 'Ye canna credit it, can ye?'

'Did he write onything else?'

'Love Letters in the Dubs.'

'Anither flop?' said Sandy.

'Athoot trace,' confirmed Erchie. 'Same wi "You're the Cream in my Brosebowl", "How Are Things in New Pitsligo?" and "I'm Dreaming of a White Charolais".'

'Isn't it funny how some things jist dinna tak a trick?' said Fobbie.

'So ye can imagine how he wis at the end o his rope, the boy,' said Erchie. 'Especially, fan he saw affa similar tunes sellin millions aa ower the warld.'

'So, excuse me for askin,' said Gibby, 'bit how come ye saved his life?'

'I wis ower at Abyne helpin them oot wi the railway in 1957,' said Erchie, 'and I'd an oor tae spare so I took a tekkie up til the boy's fairm for aul times' sake.

'Fan I got there, the din wis something affa. What a racket comin oot o the fairmhoose. Ye'd hiv thocht somebody wis bein chokit.'

'So I burst in, and I up the stairs twa at a time and there's the boy wreckin the place. His hale face wis twistit wi rage. He wis jist in an affa state wi himsel. He wis shoutin that he wis endin it aa. His sangs wis jist rubbish and he'd nithing left worth livin for.

'He ran past me doon the stairs, knocking picters affa the wa and ca'in ower the hallstand and then he ran ben til the scullery and he startit flingin cheirs oot the windae and coupin the table and rippin doon the curtains.

'Then, as true as I'm stannin here, he liftit the fridge and flung it oot the door, and it tumbled doon the fairm close and endit it up in the midden.

'Fan I lookit back, he hid a knife til his belly. I telt him nae tae be hasty. I said there wis a lot left worth livin for. He said he jist lived for his sangs, and naebody cared aboot them. He said he'd lost his inspiration and athoot inspiration, he couldna write sangs and athoot sangs he wis feenished.

'I telt him there wis inspiration in aathing if only he lookit. I telt him that if he jist held gyaun, his next song wid be the warld success he'd been waitin for.'

'Div ye think so?' he said. And I said I wis certain. So I took him oot the door tae prove ma point. And he lookit roon the fairm close and he saw the byre and the barn and the binder and then he saw the fridge that he'd thrown in the midden and his little facie lichtit up and he ran back inside for a pencil and paper and he began writin his next sang.'

'That's it,' he said. 'That's it.'

'And it wis a success?' said Fobbie.

'No, it wis a flop, tee.'

'Fit wis it caaed?'

'The Slurry with the Fridge on Top.'

8 *Anniversary Tantrums*

HAD Sandy Brose been a little more attuned to the finer feelings of women, he would have known what the problem was a little sooner than he did.

He sat in his customary Saturday-morning pose, slumped in the fireside easy chair, mug of stewed tea at his side and the racing pages of that morning's *Press and Journal* spread before him, oblivious to the curious clumping of his wife, Geneva, as she stormed round the room, dusting furiously.

When the vacuum cleaner was switched on, he looked up to scowl, intending this to demonstrate to Geneva that the sudden noise had interrupted his concentration, but Geneva's jaw was set firm as she pushed and tugged the cleaner up and down the carpet with all the vigour of a prop forward on domestic duties.

When Sandy saw that his silent protest was not working, he simply returned to studying form.

When Geneva saw that her husband seemed unperturbed, she shot the cleaner across to where the pages of the newspaper covered the fireside rug and ran it over them. They crumpled and tore instantly.

'Hie!' shouted Sandy, sitting upright. 'That's ma paper, that!'

Geneva affected surprise. 'Yer paper?' she shouted above the din. Then she looked down. 'Oh, what a peety,' she said. 'I wisna expectin a paper aa ower the fleer. I jist assumed that maist normal fowk reads the paper in their hauns. Affa sorry.'

Sandy tugged three sheets of newsprint from the jaws of the cleaner and made a show of trying to smooth them out and put them back in order, but it was clear, to Geneva's immense satisfaction, that much of the racing card was beyond repair.

Sandy folded the remains of the daily and stuffed them down the side of the chair.

Geneva, meanwhile, switched off the cleaner.

Husband studied wife as she picked up the duster and stepped across the front of him to dust the mantelpiece. In the course of the manoeuvre, she stepped on his toes twice, knocked his hand off the arm of the chair and toppled the standard lamp so that the shade bounced off his head. None of the accidents seemed to be particularly accidental, thought Sandy, but he said nothing.

'That's an affa envelopes ahen the clock,' snapped Geneva. 'Envelopes is nae for keepin ahen the clock. We keep envelopes in the bureau in this hoose.'

'I keep them ahen the clock,' said Sandy firmly. 'That wye, I ken far aathing is.'

'Get a lotta mail, div ye?'

'A fair amount, as ye can see. I dinna wint tae be rakin throwe aul letters and stuff if I need tae find something in a hurry.'

'Aul letters,' repeated Geneva. 'Ony cards maybe?'

'Nae lately.'

'I didna think so. It's nae as if we celebrate muckle in this hoose.' She stepped back from her furious dusting, then added, as her Parthian shot: 'Appeerently.'

The bang of the kitchen door merely reinforced Sandy's impression that something was up.

If their daughter, Floretta, had been at home, he could have asked her. As it was, he would have to get to the root of the problem by himself and then, assuming that he managed, he would have to try to reach some sort of appeasement.

Geneva wasn't an easy appease.

Sandy appeared in the kitchen just as Geneva was beginning to scrape carrots for the broth. He stopped beside her.

'Ye're in ma licht,' she barked. 'I canna see fit I'm deein.'

Sandy wondered how much light was necessary to scrape a carrot accurately but, wisely, said nothing. He stepped back.

'Did ye sleep aaricht?' he asked as nonchalantly as he could.

'In the circumstances.' (scrape-scrape-scrape-scrape-scrape)

'Nithing troublin ye?'

'Wid it worry ye if there wis?' (scrape-scrape-scrape-scrape)

'I jist like tae be sure noo and again that we're jaikin aaricht.'

'You tell me.' (scrape-scrape-scrape)

'Nae trouble as far's I ken.'

'Well, that'll jist be dandy, will it nae?' (scrape-scrape)

30

He sighed. 'I'm nae playin games, Geneva,' he said. 'If there's something wrang, tell me.'

'Not a thing's wrang.' (scrape) 'Not' (scrape) 'a' (scrape) 'thing' (scrape) 'is' (scrape) 'WRANG!' At the last word, she clattered the vegetable knife down on the worktop and turned to glare at him.

'Fine,' said Sandy, and he turned to go.

'That's it,' said Geneva, 'ye nivver listen tae me.'

Sandy stopped at the door. 'Ye've jist telt me nithing's wrang.'

'Ye're affa easy satisfied wi answers, aren't ye?' snapped Geneva. She turned back to her carrots.

Sandy walked back towards the sink.

'Ye're in ma licht,' she said, lifting another carrot from the basin.

He stepped back a little. 'Ye've telt me nithing's wrang,' he said. 'I've speired if we're jaikin aaricht. I've speired if there's onything troublin ye. Fit mair am I supposed tae say?'

'Ye dinna mean it, though,' said Geneva.

Sandy lowered his head and sighed deeply. 'I canna pit up wi this,' he said quietly. Then he looked up again. 'Ye're obviously in een o yer moods. There's something ye're nae tellin me and I canna guess fit it is. I'm nae Houdini. Ye'll tell me eventually, I ken that. It wid jist be a lot easier on aabody concerned if ye wid tell me noo. Ye'd raither ging throwe anither day o yer silly rigmaroles and then we'll get tae the boddim o't. Please yersel.'

Geneva thrust a half-scraped carrot and the vegetable knife into the sink and turned to her husband. The set of her hands on her hips told even someone as thick-skinned as Sandy that all was not well.

'Fit day is't the morn?' she said.

'Sunday.'

'And fit day's that?'

'The day o rest.'

'Fit day is it tae us? You and me.'

'Sunday,' said Sandy.

'Fit *special* day?'

Sandy blanched. 'It's nae yer birthday is it?'

'Ye ken fine it's nae ma birthday. Ye ken fine ma birthday's in July.'

'It's nae *my* birthday, is it?'

'It's wir anniversary,' said Geneva. She said the word so quietly that it dripped with menace.

'I'm affa sorry,' said Sandy. 'Ye should hiv said.'

'Not only is it wir anniversary,' said Geneva. 'It's a special anniversary.'

'Fit wye special?'

'It's wir thirtieth anniversary. Thirty years o wedded warfare.'

'That's fairly special,' agreed Sandy. 'And fit's the present ye wis supposed tae get?'

'Pearls,' said Geneva. 'Thirty's the pearl anniversary.'

'So fit wis the twinty-fifth, again?'

'That wis silver. Or, at least, it wis supposed tae be. Ye forgot it, as weel.'

'So if twinty-five's silver and thirty's pearl, fit wis twinty?'

'China,' said Geneva. 'Anither miss fae ye.'

'Pearl, silver and china,' mused Sandy. 'There's surely an affa special anniversaries on the go.'

'For some fowk,' said Geneva. 'Some wives hiv built up a richt fine collection o stuff for their front-room cabinets. There's memories. There's warm feelins. Thon wives can dee their dustin and think happy thochts o their younger days and aa the fine times the twa o them hid thegither. Me? I hinna enough for a bedside table.'

'Fit's the different anniversaries, like?' inquired Sandy.

'Ten's tin,' said Geneva. 'Five's widd. The first anniversary's cotton. Ye forgot the lot. In aa the time we've been mairriet, ye've minded not one single anniversary. Nae present. Nae card. Nae even a mornin kiss. For thirty year, ye hinna shiftit yersel aboot the maist inportant day in wir lives. And that's fit hurts, Sandy. Nae sae muckle the presents. It's the fact that it hisna even crossed yer mind. Not once.'

'So if I've missed aa that big anniversaries,' said Sandy. 'Fit'll wir fortieth anniversary be?'

Geneva turned back to her carrots. 'A miracle.'

9 Kate's Diet Despair

THE laughter, chatter and general melée of the annual Stronach Show was nowhere noisier than at the village hall, where the women of the WRI had set themselves up as usual offering teas, homebakes and savoury snacks. Despite the fact that it was at least half a mile from the showpark, the women always did a roaring trade, and this year's show was no exception. If anything, the hall seemed to be even more bustling than usual and trade did not begin to die off until well after 4pm.

By 5pm, when the last of stragglers, belching and holding straining bellies, had manoeuvred themselves through the door, the WRI women were left with a familiar scene of devastation and detritus.

'I dinna ken fit wye we bother,' said Babbie Girn. 'Nivver a thank-you or nithing. They jist bore in lik gannets, jaas goin lik the clappers fit for twinty minutes, then they leave. They dinna tak time.'

'Never you mind, Mrs Girn,' said WRI president Kate Barrington-Graham. 'The very fact that we are so well patronised on this annual occasion of festivities attests surely to the esteem in which our culinary aspirations are held, would you not concur?'

'The very words oot o ma moo,' said Geneva Brose.

'Weel,' said Aggie Dreep, surveying the surplus, 'we maybe did a roarin trade, bit there's still eneuch left that wid feed an army. Fit'll we dee wi aa this grub? We canna fling it oot.'

Babbie Girn reached for the big brown-enamel teapot. 'Weel, ladies,' she said. 'I dinna ken aboot you, bit I've been on ma feet aa day, and I'm sair needin a cuppie and a fine piece, so if ye dinna mind I'll awa and mak masel a weel-deserved fly. Onybody else?'

A clamour from a dozen WRI women told Babbie that the demand for a relaxing fly cup and some of the remains of the day was universal, so she swapped the medium-sized teapot for the large, economy model and trotted off to the kitchen.

As three of the women began sorting the remains of fancy cakes, biscuits, traybakes, sausage rolls and sandwiches into some order, Aggie, Flo and Mrs Barrington-Graham collapsed, exhausted, on a trestle bench against the far wall.

'Well,' said Mrs Barrington-Graham. 'If we haven't cleared at least £400 for institute funds, I'll be very surprised. It makes all the aches and pains seem worthwhile somehow.'

'Are ye bathered wi aches and pains, like?' inquired Aggie.

'Terribly. Just terribly. You know, they seem to have crept up on me all of a sudden. Creaky joints. Knees that snap when I stand up. Stiff neck if I fall asleep in the wing chair. Incessant squeaking from elbows, hips and ankles. Life's such a trial.'

'Nivver you mind, Mrs Barrington-Graham,' said Flo. 'Here comes Babbie wi the tae. Ye'll seen forget yer aches and pains wi a bit cream sponge and a twa–three meltin moments in yer intimmers.'

'Oh, no, no, no,' squealed Mrs Barrington-Graham. 'I couldn't possibly.'

'Couldna hae a funcy piece?' said three women. 'Efter you workin amon them aa day?'

'I'd absolutely love to,' said Mrs Barrington-Graham, 'but I daren't. I seem to be going through such a difficult dietary phase at the moment. The pounds just pile on. I can't fit into my Antonia Cinquetti or my Pfeiffenberger at all now.'

'I ken foo ye feel,' Geneva said. 'My Pfeiffenberger's been up in the laft for wikks. Canna dee nithing wi't.'

'It's so dispiriting,' said Mrs Barrington-Graham. 'Life's such a trial.'

'Well, it wid be dispiritin,' said Aggie. 'You and yer Antonia thing and yer Foffenbugger. Here's me wi a Littlewoods frock that's real tucky.'

'The devil of it is that I can't find a diet plan that works. I've tried the banana diet. I've tried the graprefruit diet. I've tried the Beverly Hills Diet. Atkins. F-Plan. J-Plan. D-Plan. You name it, it doesn't work for me. I've even tried the O-Plan diet in last month's *Woman's Globe* magazine.'

'The O-Plan diet,' Aggie said.

'The O-Plan,' said Mrs Barrington-Graham. 'The O stands for oil. You're supposed to supplement each meal with a tablespoon of whatever cooking oil you happen to have in the house. Olive is best, but you can substitute corn oil, vegetable oil, sunflower oil or rapeseed oil.'

Babbie and the other WRI ladies stared, not entirely sure if Mrs Barrington-Graham was pulling their legs. Mrs Barrington-Graham simply looked back, unblinking.

'Ye're tellin's that if ye pit raa cookin ile ower yer grub, ye loase weicht?' Babbie said.

Mrs Barrington-Graham nodded.

'Awa ye go,' Babbie said. 'Ile's pure calories. Ye'd be as weel ging on a cream-meringue diet.'

'Seriously,' Mrs Barrington-Graham said. 'It's something to do with restricting the energy uptake by putting a barrier lining of suspension lipids on the stomach.'

'Hiv ye tried this diet?' Babbie said.

Mrs Barrington-Graham nodded.

'And dis't work?' Geneva said.

'Not that I can notice,' Mrs Barrington-Graham said. 'I'm not any thinner at all.'

'I'm nae surprised,' Geneva said.

'Nivver you mind, Mrs Barrington-Graham,' piped up Dorothy Birze. 'Even though it's nae workin, look on the bricht side.'

'The bright side?' said Mrs Barrington-Graham.

'Aye,' Dorothy said. 'Though ye're maybe nae ony thinner, keep it up a whilie langer and yer jints'll stop squeakin.'

10 *Sammy Dreams Dreams*

IT was quiet in the centre of the village, even for a Monday morning. Erchie Sotter had watched a puckle tractors and a lorry or two rumbling through the village in half an hour, but nothing else to speak of.

A few hardy souls were braving the unseasonal chill, happit against the wind blowing off the Hill of Stronach, but clearly many more were staying by their firesides, and wisely so. Erchie reflected for a moment on how soft the North-east had become since his own young day.

Then he spied young Sammy Dreep emerging from the savings bank across the street.

'Sammy,' cried Erchie. 'Come awa and gie's yer news.'

Sammy strode to the kerb and checked this way and that for traffic, although he needn't have bothered, and strode towards the old green bench where Erchie was seated.

'Awa in depositin anither million, wis ye?' said Erchie.

'No,' said Sammy. 'I hinna got a million, ye see.'

Erchie mused that Sammy would never have much of a facility at banter.

'I wis in checkin ma accoont,' explained Sammy, plonking himself down. 'I'm nae makkin muckle progress. I doot I winna be startin the college efter the summer. Nae unless the premium bonds come up.'

'Hiv ye premium bonds, like?'

'No.'

Erchie rubbed his chin. 'Kinna limits yer horizons, that.'

'I'm mair or less resigned til ma fate,' said Sammy. 'I canna see me ivver gettin oot o this hole.'

'I beg yer pardon? This hole?'

'The village. Stronach. I can see me bein stuck here aa ma days. Ither fowk traivel the globe and mak their pile, and I'll be here swipin the streets or stuck ahen a shop coonter til the day I retire.'

'And fit's wrang wi that? That's perfectly respectable wyes tae mak a half-croon. There's plenty fowk nooadays wid be gled o the chunce.'

'Nae me, Erchie. I've ma dreams. I've ma hopes. Bidin at Stronach disna figure in ony o them.'

'I've heard some bigsy things in ma time,' said Erchie. 'Bit I nivver thocht I'd hear sic rubbish fae you. Fa are you that ye've risen abeen yer station? Are ye denyin yer reets?'

'Nithing adee wi station or reets,' said Sammy. 'It's jist a fact, plain and simple. Some fowk likes bidin in the same place aa their days. I'm fed up o't. I've itchy feet.'

'Awa ower and see the chemist, than.'

Sammy turned to sit side-on, facing Erchie on the bench. 'It's aaricht for you, Erchie,' he said. 'You've seen the world. Ye've seen maist o Europe wi the war and things. Ye've lived. I hinna hardly kent nithing bit here and The Toon and the road atween the twa. And here's me twenty-five. There's fowk makkin their second million at twenty-five, Erchie. I canna even mak ma second hunner.'

'Twenty-five's nae past it,' began Erchie.

'I mean, are you nae sometimes annoyed wi the rubbish that fowk in sma villagies pit up wi?'

'Rubbish?' said Erchie.

'The nonsense. The trivia. If I hear ma mither jist one mair gettin hersel workit up aboot the icin on her chocolate sponge for some WRI competition, I think I'll awa and tak a blue peel. Fa cares aboot chocolate sponges? Fa's interestit in whether the icin's saft or soor? Is this aa they've got tae fill their days? Chocolate sponges and bickerin aboot icin?

'Can they nae find something worth the worry; something worth deein wi themsels? Can they nae see they're jist markin time wi tripe till the Grim Reaper taps them on the shooder and says: 'Excuse me, Mrs Dreep, I believe it's your shottie noo.'

Erchie sat blinking at the vehemence of it all. Finally, when Sammy had wound down and was shaking his head sadly, Erchie tapped him on the shoulder.

'I think ye're some hard on yer freens,' he said. 'Ye look at them and ye see aul fowk fillin their days wi fit you think's trivia and nae worth a second look.

'I look at them and I see young lads forty or fifty year back that put

37

their backs intil jobs on the fairm, or diggin the roads or rinnin the railway and a dizzen ither things that needit deein.

'I see fowk that's raised faimlies and made sacrifices for them and consider that that's a fair contribution itsel. I see fowk that's earned their rest; fowk that kens they've deen their bit and thinks it's time ither fowk took the strain.

'You see fowk that fill their days wi rubbish, as ye ca't. Hiv you ony idea o the importance o icin on a chocolate sponge? Can ye nae see it his nithing adee wi icin or chocolate sponges. It his aathing adee wi achievement, and public recognition o skills that hiv taen decades tae perfect.

'Fit wid ye hae them dee? Brain surgery? Fleein planes? Michty, it's competitions lik that keeps them goin. Maks them think. They're nae tae be sneered at.'

'I wisna sneerin. I wis jist sayin it wisna for me.'

'And fa said they were for you, like? His onybody been at ye wi an application form for jinin the WRI? Hiv they? Is onybody askin ye tae mak a chocolate sponge? Get up aff yer backside, Sammy, and stop feelin sorry for yersel. Dee something, instead o waitin for somebody else tae dee something for ye.'

Now it was Sammy's turn to blink in the face of vehemence, and the silence that fell over him was such that Erchie worried that he had gone too far.

'Aye, weel,' said Erchie, sitting back on the bench. 'Aa I'm sayin is dinna see fowk for their age. See them for the work they've deen and fit they've achieved. Tak it fae me, ye'll get a hale new angle on them. Ye'll maybe appreciate them mair, instead o gettin workit up aboot them.'

Erchie paused for a moment, and studied a figure across the street.

'I mean,' he said, 'look at aul Fobbie Pluffer ower the road.'

Sammy raised his head and saw Fobbie making his measured way down past the bank, the chemist and the post office. There was a purposeful set about him. As far as his bad knee allowed, there was a determination in his walk.

'Fit div ye see there?' said Erchie.

'Jist Fobbie.'

'Jist Fobbie? Fit div ye mean jist Fobbie? I'll tell ye fit I see. I see a man that ran in front o a larry wi failed brakes and scoopit a young baby up intil his bosie jist afore the war and saved her life.'

'I nivver kent.'

'And that young lassie gaed by the name o Agnes Toast.'

'Ma mither?'

'So, ye see, Fobbie Pluffer maybe worries ower muckle aboot his dahlias in the gairden competition, and he maybe yatters on and on a bit much for some fowk, bit he fairly hid his uses in his younger day, widn't ye say?'

Sammy said nothing.

'And far wid ye think he's gaun noo; him stridin oot doon the road lik that?'

Sammy studied Fobbie again. 'I dinna ken,' he said.

'I ken. He's awa doon til the bobby.'

'Fit's happened?'

'He wis kidnapped by three lassies in their twinties. They knockit the feet fae under him, took him ahen a barn up at Bogensharn and hauled the claes aff him. He wisna found til the next mornin, hardly able tae spik.'

'Michty, fan did this happen?'

'The August afore the war startit.'

'And he's jist gaun til the bobbies noo?'

'No, he gaes til the bobbies ilky ither Monday aboot it.'

'Fit wye?'

'He jist likes spikkin aboot it.'

11 *Thole's Lonely Sermon*

SUNLIGHT streamed in through the bedroom window of the Rev. Montgomery Thole. One of his little habits, developed over fifty-five years, was that between Easter and Harvest Thanksgiving, he did not draw his bedroom curtains at night.

He had once told Miss Euphemia Pink, the teacher, that it did him good to have his spirits lifted before he got up, and seemed to give him more energy throughout spring and summer days.

Mr Thole lay back on his pillows, turned his head to look at the gentle green glow of the alarm clock and smiled to himself.

Today, he decided, he would preach about the simple joys; the benefits which the good Lord had provided free of charge and which, in the hurry and scurry of modern living, too many people overlooked.

He decided he would jog his congregation's memories about the pleasures in simplicity and the lack of material possessions.

Then the timer on his bedroom TV switched on, followed seconds later by the radio and, a few seconds after that, the hi-fi.

MONTGOMERY Thole bustled into his kitchen, still pink, shiny and scrubbed from his shower. He had hoped that his stand-in housekeeper, Mrs Lottie Dicht, might have arrived early to begin preparing the full Scottish breakfast he liked on Sundays, but the back door of the manse was still locked. Presumably, Mrs Dicht had had a night on the tiles and was still abed. He would have to speak to her about it.

With a glass of orange juice in his hand, he wandered through to his study, at the front of the manse, and looked out on the village.

How puzzling, he thought. Not a soul to be seen.

He turned round to look at the grandfather clock against the back wall. 8.23. Even for a Sunday, that was late enough for at least someone to be out walking a dog, or washing a car or strolling for the papers.

But there was no one.

Mr Thole downed the last of his orange juice, put the glass on a small table by the aspidistra, shuffled out of his slippers and went to get his shoes.

Out on the street, the village was just as still.

An occasional car of tourists slowed as it passed through, but always such cars picked up speed and passed on.

Mr Thole stepped up the Main Street for a few hundred yards, expecting to see someone doing a little light weeding before church or some similarly innocuous activity. But there was no one.

'It's a little like a science-fiction story,' he muttered to himself. 'The last man at Stronach.'

He turned on his heels and wandered back to the manse and the kirk. There was no one on the bench outside the bakery. No one on the circular seat round the tree at the tourist notice-board. No one at all.

He took one last look up the street, then hurried down the little brae to the manse door and went inside.

'Mrs Dicht!' he called in the lobby. 'Mrs Dicht! Are you there?'

Mrs Dicht was not there.

Mr Thole returned to his study, picked up his sermon notes and flopped into an easy chair to read through them.

Periodically, he thought he saw someone walking along the street and went to the window to peer out, but always it was an illusion.

By 10.30, it was clear that he would have to open up the church himself, which he did.

In the vestry, surrounded by the glum, scowling faces of his predecessors, he donned his vestments and, occasionally, peered out into the church itself.

Several times, he imagined he heard cars, but when he poked his head out of the vestry's outer door, he saw no car.

More importantly, he saw no congregation.

'And no organist,' he said to himself. 'No Miss Pink.'

Montgomery Thole had not conducted a service without an organist before.

'They'll have to hum,' he told himself. 'It works on the West Coast. There's no reason why it can't work here.'

As the minute hand on the old Glasgow clock clacked round to the hour, he opened the vestry door and strode into the church.

There was only one other person in the entire building.

Mr Thole took off his reading glasses, swapped them for his other pair and peered out.

It was the farmer from Bogensharn. How ironic, thought Mr Thole, that on a day when none of his trusted regulars had turned out, a man who barely made it for one communion a year had appeared.

Mr Thole paused for a moment in the pulpit, shuffling his notes, then stepped down.

As he walked up the church, Bogies eyed him warily.

'Helloooo,' said Mr Thole in what he imagined was a soothing, welcoming tone. 'How very nice to see you here.'

'Ye're nae exactly steerin wi fowk,' said Bogies. 'There's jist me.'

'So it seems. So it seems. Um, what do you suppose has happened? Has everyone else been abducted by aliens? Ha ha ha.'

Bogies eyed Mr Thole. 'Nivver an alien, meenister,' he said. 'Ye ken the Rural wis on a bus trippie tae Skye yestreen?'

'Indeed?'

'Weel, their bus broke doon on the road hame last nicht at Carrbridge. They're aa kippit up at the village hall, appeerently. The hotel fowk at Carrbridge his been affa gweed til them; feedin them soup and aathing.'

'Oh, how dreadful. How do you know this?'

'The wife's stucken there wi them. What a rare nicht I hid last nicht.'

'But that's the Rural. What about the menfolk?'

'Some kinna golf medal at Gleneagles. There's twa busloads awa til that.'

'So I'm left with just you?'

'Weel, if ye're nae sikkin me . . .'

'I meant nothing like that, I do assure you. Please, don't be offended. But, my goodness, I don't think I've ever had such a bizarre Sunday morning in my entire life.'

He paused for a moment.

'Tell me, do you hum?'

'Ach, it's likely the nowt. I canna get the stink o skitter aff me for love nor . . .'

'No, no, no. Do you hum as in singing? We don't have an organist, you see. I assume Miss Pink is stuck at Carrbridge, too, although I'm a little miffed that she didn't think to phone.'

'I'm nae muckle o a hummer, no.'

'Tell me, in that case, do you think I should go ahead with the sermon at all?'

Bogies thought for a moment, then looked up. 'Meenister,' he said. 'If I tak a bucket o seed til ma hens and only ae hen turns up, I dinna pit it awa hungry.'

Mr Thole brightened. 'I say,' he said. 'How very apt. You realise you've just told me a parable. I shall use that at some point in the future Mr . . . um . . . Mr . . .'

'Jist ca me Bogies. Aabody else dis.'

'Mr Bogies. Yes. Right-o, let's proceed.'

TRULY, it was a bizarre service. The singing was limited to Mr Thole's over-trebly tenor and an agricultural grunt in every second line from Bogies.

The prayers echoed more than usual.

But the sermon pushed the boundary a little too much. Working on the basis that a rare attendee had better hear the works, Mr Thole laboured points which normally he would have passed off lightly. He seemed oblivious to Bogies nodding gently towards slumber and snapping awake again whenever Mr Thole banged the pulpit with his palm. He was blind to the increasing frequency of Bogies glancing at his watch.

When, eventually, the ordeal was over, and Bogies had climbed out of the pew to go, Mr Thole scurried down the aisle and drew up behind his one-man audience.

'Thank you so much for attending,' he said. 'It would have been rather a lonely morning without you.'

'Aye, richt enough.'

'I do so hope that you enjoyed it and that we'll see you again soon. Um, don't be a stranger, as they say.'

'No.'

'Um, tell me, Mr Bogies, you did enjoy the sermon, didn't you?'

Bogies turned. 'Pit it this wye, meenister,' he said, 'Ye ken how I said that if I tak a bucket o seed til ma hens and only ae hen turns up, I dinna pit it awa hungry?'

'Yes.'

'Weel, if only ae hen comes for feedin, I dinna gie her the hale pail fae.'

43

12 *Gibby, Wedding Usher*

FLO Spurtle leaned back against the sink and took another sip of her tea. As she sipped, she watched her husband, rushing this way and that, hunting for things which were not lost and carrying things back and forth which would have been better left in one spot. Presently, Gibby stopped, face flushed and hair dishevelled, and glared at her as she stood there, sipping her tea.

'Ye're busy?' he snapped.

She lowered the cup and smiled. 'Gibby, this is nae my problem. I'm jist a guest at this waddin. It's you that agreed tae be an usher. It's you that needs tae be at the kirk an oor afore onybody else. I speired at ye last nicht if ye needit onything laid oot and ye said aathing wis in hand. Now look at ye. Ye've been rinnin back and fore here for twinty minutes and ye've a face lik a turkey cock.'

'That's nae the pint,' said Gibby. 'The pint is I could hardly get oot o deein a favour for ma cousin. The ither pint is I dinna like gettin dressed up lik a penguin. And the final pint is that if ee've an oor afore ye need tae dress, ye could gie me a hand.'

'Is that a request?' said Flo.

Gibby glared at her again.

'Only I didna hear the magic word.'

'Please,' said Gibby.

Flo put her tea down on the worktop. 'Aaricht,' she said. 'Gie's yer sheen for cleanin.' Gibby raced to the gloryhole for his best black Oxfords. 'Though I must say,' said Flo, 'that ye're a bittie aul for usherin. It's usually laddies still at the school that get that job. I hope ye're nae bein set up for a lachin stock.'

FLO took one last look at herself in the hallstand mirror and congratulated herself on her good taste. The bus trip to Turriff for a new outfit had paid dividends, and she simply knew that people would be noticing and commenting favourably behind her back.

Another toot at the front door hurried her along. She grabbed her hat and gloves from the hallstand table and made for the front door.

Outside in a taxi sat Babbie Girn and Virginia Huffie – Babbie scowling in front and Virginia neat and composed in the back.

Flo hurried down the path and climbed into the back of the taxi beside Virginia. 'This is affa good o ye,' she peched as she settled herself.

The taxi pulled away.

'Gibby wis lookin real smart,' said Virginia, clapping Flo's hand gently. 'I saw him fae ma front room as he drove past. Real smart.'

'Div ye think so?' said Flo. 'I hope so. He's nae affa good in public and I widna like him showin himsel up. Ma only worry is that he taks something for his nerves and it disna 'gree wi him.'

'Is he allergic tae peels?' said Virginia.

'Nae peels,' said Flo. 'I'm thinkin mair o the dangers o a liquid cure for his nerves.'

'Surely no,' said Babbie from the front seat. 'He widna nip in past a pub fin he's himsel.'

'He's nae himsel,' said Flo. 'That's the pint. He's wi Erchie.'

There was a silence for a few moments.

'Peer quine,' muttered Babbie.

They drew up to the Inverspaver West Kirk in good time, and Babbie instructed the taxi driver to sit for a few moments so that they could get a decent view of the other outfits as they entered the kirk. At a suitable lull in proceedings, Babbie thanked the driver and paid him the fare showing on the meter, without tip, and hauled herself from the taxi.

She crochled and hobbled for a few seconds until the stiffness in her joints eased and then, hooking herself into Virginia's arm, she led the trio across the road.

'Dinna worry, Flo,' said Virginia. 'I ken by foo quaet ye are that ye're worried, bit if I ken your Gibby, he'll rise tae the occasion. Mark my words, in anither oor ye'll be richt prood o him.'

'Ye'd think he wis performin a brain operation at For'sterhill or something,' muttered Babbie. 'He's jist pintin fowk ae wye or anither. A bloomin traffic licht.'

THEY heard Gibby before they saw him. His voice seemed louder somehow, and Flo's apprehensiveness grew with every step the queue took forward to the door of the kirk.

She managed to catch a few words. 'Ye're lookin richt bonnie', appeared to be part of his ushering repertoire. 'Ye should be in the fillims', was another. 'Is that yer ain frock or are ye jist brakkin't in for Jennifer Lopez?' was third-favourite.

By the time Babbie, Virginia and Flo had negotiated the vestibule, Flo was fearing the worst. Even Virginia's platitudes and reassurances had ceased.

With good reason.

As they stepped into the kirk itself, they had their first proper view of Gibby, and it was not heartening.

He was upright and was not drunk, strictly speaking, but he was not quite as crisp and pristine as he had been when he had left the house two hours earlier. A certain distance was in the eyes, and suggested that Erchie had, indeed, tempted Gibby to a bar en route for something to steady his ushering nerves.

'Oxfam Shop again?' Flo heard Gibby say to the amply upholstered matron two groups in front, and she cringed.

'Ma mither hid a frock jist lik that,' Gibby was now telling the woman immediately in front. 'What a lang time it laistit.'

And then it was Flo, Babbie and Virginia's turn. Wisely, Gibby said nothing, but with the intense concentration of the intoxicated, tried to persuade them that he was 100 per cent sober.

'Freens o the groom, ladies?' he said, managing a slight bow and pointing them up the aisle. Flo shot him a wait-till-I-get-you-home glare, but Gibby was already on to the couple behind. 'Is that fruit on yer hat fresh or stuffed?'

Flo, Babbie and Virginia settled themselves in silence in the first available pew. It took a few minutes for any of them to speak. They filled the awkwardness by affecting great interest in their surroundings and in the garb of others in the congregation.

'Weel,' said Virginia at last, 'he wisna too bad really, I suppose.'

Babbie simply harumphed.

'Onywye,' said Virginia, fingering the clasp of her handbag, 'aa that I can say is that if I ivver get mairriet, I wish Gibby wid be the usher at my waddin.'

'Aye,' mumbled Flo wistfully, 'it's times like this I wish he'd been the usher at mine.'

13 *Ebenezer Considers Retiring*

EBENEZER Grip shuffled back and forth with the emporium stepladder and manoeuvred it slowly along behind the counter until he came to the appointed spot. He paused for breath then put his foot on the bottom step.

'Ye canna dee that,' said Erchie Sotter, sitting on the old wooden seat beside the shop door. 'Nae at your age. Ye're ower aul for climmin laidders.'

Ebenezer stopped and turned round. 'I dinna see nae ither blighter volunteerin,' he said. 'And the wifie Barrington-Graham's needin her order made up afore dennertime. I've nae option bit use the laidder.'

'Ye're ninety-six,' said Erchie, standing up. 'Fit wid happen if ye fell aff?'

'The same as wid happen if I wis twenty-six,' said Ebenezer.

'Na, na, na,' said Erchie, striding across. 'Ye canna dee that. Let me.'

He lifted the flap and walked behind the counter to grip the base of the ladder. Ebenezer looked for a moment as if he might be about to argue, but he stood aside without saying anything, leaving Erchie's way clear.

Erchie began his ascent gingerly, but considerably more sure-footed than his chum, two decades older. Presently, he returned to earth and handed Ebenezer two cards of ribbon and a bottle of paraffin perfume.

Ebenezer made to take them, but Erchie held on tightly. 'Ebenezer,' he said, 'is it nae aboot time ye took yer rest?'

'Fly time's anither twenty minutes yet,' said Ebenezer.

'That's nae fit I mean, and weel ye ken it,' said Erchie. 'Tak yer rest. Pit yer feet up. Enjoy fit's left til ye. Ninety-six is ower aul for workin day in, day oot.'

Ebenezer stood back from the ladder and glared at Erchie. 'And fit's brocht this on?' he said sharply, his hand still outstretched to receive the ribbon and perfume

'Watchin ye pechin aboot wi that laidder for a start,' said Erchie.'

Ebenezer, propped himself against the counter and thought deeply. Then he sighed. 'Tell ye the truth,' he said, running a hand over his thinning hair, 'I've been winderin aboot jackin it in for a filie noo. I am gettin affa tired whiles. The only trouble is, I canna think fa wid tak ower the shop. Neen o the femly's interested.'

'Sell the shop,' said Erchie. 'Dinna bather wi the femly. They're nae interestit. Get yer siller oot and enjoy a retirement as lang's ye can. Look efter number one for a change.'

'Canna sell the shop,' said Ebenezer. 'It's a femly tradition. There's been a Grip in this shop for near twa centuries. I canna let it go jist lik that.'

'Excuse me for sayin,' said Erchie, 'Bit I dinna think ye'll be keepin tradition goin muckle langer whither ye sell the shop or no. Ye're better gettin the good o yer time as lang's ye can.'

'The wye ye're spikkin, ye'd think I wis on the road oot completely,' said Ebenezer. 'Michty, I've ma health. There's naebody healthier in the vale than me.'

'I'm nae doubtin ye for a meenit,' said Erchie. 'I canna mind the last time ye'd as muckle as a caul. Bit that canna go on for ivver. Better cry aff noo fin it's still yer ain decision, than cry aff because ye're strappit up in a hospital bed.'

Ebenezer paused, as if giving the matter serious thought.

'I hiv been feeling a puckle aches and pains lately, richt enough,' he conceded. 'And it is gettin a bittie harder gettin oot o ma bed in the mornins. I've often funcied a lang lie bit, ach, ye get intil a routine.'

'Time for a new routine,' said Erchie. 'Fit aboot it?'

'Afore I'm conniched aathegiether?'

Erchie nodded.

Ebenezer thought again, then a smile broke over his craggy features.

'Fit's the joke?' said Erchie.

'I wis jist thinkin aboot the only time I nearly endit up in hospital.'

'The beer larry?' said Erchie.

'Aye, the beer larry. The year o the Great Gale – '53, wis't? – and

48

you and me's stannin oot the back takkin delivery o a load o ale and stuff aff the back o the beer larry.'

'And ye slippit aneth the larry wheels,' said Erchie.

'And you clattered the driver's door that hard ti warn him that he got a fleg and his fit slippit aff the clutch and ran ower baith yer feet.'

'So then you ran roon and battered on his ither door and jist bamboozled him completely, and he crunched it intae gear that hard that he loupit forrit and a hale pile o crates fell aff the side o the flatbed and ye jist aboot disappeared in crates and burstin bottles.'

'Nae funny,' laughed Erchie. 'I wis in hospital near twa wikks efter that. Great big, hivvy things, lemonade crates in them days. Solid widd. I'd a broken leg and a broken haun ower the heids o you and that ale delivery.'

'Aye,' said Ebenezer, 'a historic day, richt enough.'

'Fit div ye mean "a historic day"?'

'Weel, think aboot it,' said Ebenezer. 'In aa the time I've kent ye, that one day in 1953's the only time it's happened.'

'The only time fit's happened?'

'That wis the only time the drink's been on you.'

14 *Crochlie Neuk Concert*

IT was the clipboard that made Kate Barrington-Graham look so officious, the staff at Crochlie Neuk Eventide Home decided. The deputy manager at the home didn't care much for the woman in any case, but that clipboard which Mrs Barrington-Graham brandished so proudly opened up whole new avenues of detestation.

'They'll soon be ready out in the garden, Mrs Barrington-Graham,' said the deputy care manager, gently cupping Mrs Barrington-Graham's elbow.

'That might very well be,' said Mrs Barrington-Graham, scanning the top two sheets of paper on her board, 'but until I am ready in here, we won't be doing anything very much at all, will we?'

So the deputy care manager just shrugged her shoulders and turned to walk away down the main lobby. She knew the idea of a Guy Fawkes fireworks display and concert party was questionable the minute matron had proposed it. When she discovered that matron had not been particularly keen, either, and had succumbed to weeks of relentless pressure by Mrs Barrington-Graham, she had tried to wash her hands of it, to little avail.

Mrs Barrington-Graham's keenness for good community works was stoked by Mrs Barrington-Graham's need to be revered.

The deputy care manager went into the day room where twenty-two residents were ranked in a wide semi-circle in an assortment of chairs. It was dark outside already, but the drapes had not been drawn. Outside, floodlit on the lawn, Gibby Spurtle was putting the finishing touches to rows of launch tubes that would have done credit to a small Atlantic destroyer, but all of this was lost on the residents, who read their papers or played with their sleeves or sat in wing chairs snoring.

'Come away now, ladies and gentlemen,' said the deputy care manager, clapping her hands gently. 'It'll soon be time for the show to start and you won't want to miss anything. Not after all the hard work by Mr Spurtle and the ladies of the WRI.'

'Is Cilla Black dae od yet?' asked Mina Drabb, dabbing her hankie against a heavy cold and scowling from one end of a sofa towards a blank TV.

'But you're getting something much more interesting tonight than Cilla Black, Mina,' said the deputy care manager. 'It's fireworks and a WRI concert party.'

'Whoop-de-do,' snochered Mina.

There was a tap on the french windows. The deputy care manager walked across and opened them to Gibby. He handed her a reel of cable. 'Could ye tak this ben and sit it next tae that keyboard thing against the back wa?' he said. 'I'll come in in five minties and wire it up. Foo's the wifie Barrington-Graham?'

'Anxious to start.'

'Tell here I winna be minutes. I'll jist check the last connections at the boords and the tubes and that'll be me.'

'You're the boss,' said the deputy care manager, shrugging her shoulders.

IN FACT, Gibby took fully ten minutes before he had done his last checks and wired up the keyboard launcher that the fireworks company had provided. With almost forty white keys for the rocket sequences, and thirty black keys for the assorted static fireworks, it was a complicated job and it had to be done properly and safely.

'Nivver mind,' he told himself as he cross-checked the last connection against the wiring diagram, 'it'll mak a rare finale.'

At last, he stood upright and gave a thumbs-up to the deputy care manager who was waiting by the door. She turned to look down the corridor and also gave a thumbs-up, then she turned down the dimmer switch for the day-room lighting and turned up the switch for the spotlights on the small stage.

'Ladies and gentlemen,' said a voice booming through the speakers with whistle and feedback, 'a big hand please for the Stronach WRI concert party.' Four residents clapped, seventeen turned to look at the stage and one soul in an easy chair away at the back carried on snoring.

Nine of the WRI ladies came on to the stage, peering against the spotlights into the blackness where their audience lurked. Virginia Huffie sat down at the piano towards the side of the stage and hammered out the opening chords of "Annie Laurie".

Over the next three minutes, Geneva Brose did an effective job of mangling one of Scotland's most beautiful melodies and received a slow handclap for her pains.

This was followed by a five-minute comedy playlet which was received in heavy silence, a bothy ballad by 'guest artistes' Sandy Brose and Walter Dreep which raised only groans and a cry from somewhere in the darkness of: 'Is Cilla Black dae od yet?', and a stand-up comedy set by Aggie Dreep which drew not even a smile.

Now, three residents were snoring.

Mrs Barrington-Graham was scowling from the wings. 'Don't be downcast, ladies; don't be downcast,' she muttered from behind her clipboard. 'Some people just don't appreciate good, clean entertainment.'

'We telt ye wikks ago that this wis a waste o time,' said Babbie Girn. 'Aul fowk's mair sophisticatit nooadays, but wid ye listen? Ye widna listen. We're nae downcast in the least. It's you that's left wi egg on yer face, ye . . . ye . . . *wifie.*'

At which point Babbie and the entire cast went out on to the stage for a country-dancing demonstration.

Alas, the vibrations of almost a dozen burly Stronach residents battering heavily round a makeshift stage set up such vibrations that no one noticed Virginia Huffie and her piano-stool edging closer and closer to the edge of the platform. The dance was scarcely half done when the stool finally tipped, sending Virginia three feet below, grasping curtains and pulling the curtain-poles out of the ceiling and wrapping the dancers in drapes and cardboard scenery.

There was a huge burst of applause from the audience. Two of the snorers woke up with a start.

Mrs Barrington-Graham appeared on stage as the dancers extricated themselves from the remains of soft-furnishings, while two care assistants led a hirpling Virginia away to a treatment room.

Mrs Barrington-Graham peered out to the applause in the blackness. 'Quiet,' she barked. 'Quiet. We're coming to our last act, a singsong, but we're short of a pianist now. Can any of you play the piano?'

Mina Drabb shot out of her seat. 'I'll dirl a key or twa for ye,' she said, ramming her sodden hankie up her sleeve and scuttling across the room.

But Mina headed not for the upright at which Virginia had been seated. Instead, she arrived three feet sooner at the fireworks key-board that Gibby had finished setting up half an hour earlier.

' "The black and white rag", by Winifred Atwell!' Mina announced, and she began hammering out the up-tempo tune that had been so popular in the '50s.

Within seconds, the room was filled with a flood of coloured light as hundreds of pounds worth of rockets, catherine wheels, roman candles, Chinese lanterns, skyflashes and starbursts went off simul-taneously.

The residents, wide-eyed and silent, gaped at the display outside while Mina, tapping her feet, shaking her head in time and hammer-ing the keyboard, seemed oblivious to the fact that no sound emanated from her 'piano'.

Gibby, the home staff and the concert party stared for the entire twenty seconds that their firework display lasted, and said nothing even when the last of the coloured lights faded and died and the dayroom returned to darkness, although someone fancied they heard quiet sobbing from Mrs Barrington-Graham.

An hour later, as the concert party began leaving, smiling and shaking hands with the residents, and pecking them on the cheek, they reflected on the fact that Crochlie Neuk had had its best Guy Fawkes night in years.

As Mrs Barrington-Graham steeled herself to shake hands with Mina Drabb, she managed to say through clenched teeth: 'I believe you have a bad cold. I hope you get better soon.'

Mina replied: 'Thank ye. We aa hope yer concerts get better, tee.'

15 *Babbie's New Shower*

BABBIE Girn was idly stirring her tea, enjoying the sunshine as she sat in the bay window of the Cozy Cuppie Cafe, the new tearoom in the middle of Stronach. The turn of April into May always cheered her, and the weather today was certainly not letting her down.

Babbie turned to look at the wall clock and noted that it was a few minutes before ten. She could stay for another twenty minutes before she would have to hurry home to let in the tradesmen.

Today was a big day. After years of climbing in and out of the enamel bath that had been installed when her house had been built, she was spending a little of her savings on a new bathroom suite.

She had mentioned it to no one. Well, it was no one's business. She knew they would be peering from their windows, anyway, as the various vans and pick-ups arrived and all the old fittings were carried down the garden path and taken away.

No matter. The money was hers. She was perfectly entitled to spend it without reference to anyone else.

Only one thing troubled Babbie: she had opted for a shower with a seat, rather than a bath with one of those little wall-mounted hoists for lowering the occupant into the water. Aul age disna come itsel, and Babbie had been noticing more and more difficulty in getting easily and comfortably into her old bath. A shower, she had decided, would be the answer. A fine big shower. Not one of those poky wee cubicles on a plastic tray, without enough room to raise your elbows. Something you could move about in and ablute all the important little places without banging your head on the tiles.

Babbie peeled the wrapper off her Kit-Kat and was just about to take the first bite, happy to think that life would be a little easier for her shortly, when she spied a form on the other side of the street. It was the Rev. Montgomery Thole.

Babbie tried to retreat into her coat, but enjoying the sunshine in the bay window had its price and Mr Thole soon spotted her and gave her a cheery wave.

Babbie managed a weak wave back and then looked down at the tablecloth, pretending she was reading something of grave import. She peered upwards as surreptitiously as she could and noticed that Mr Thole had taken four or five steps more but, alas, had stopped. He was crossing the street.

Babbie sat upright, resigned to an encounter. She brushed a few crumbs from her coat and managed a thin smile as the bell on the café door pinged and Mr Thole poked his head round.

'Mrs Girn,' he said brightly, as if she had returned that very morning from thirty years' exile in the South Seas. 'How very nice to see you.' He shut the door and stepped across. 'Do you mind if I join you?'

Babbie motioned him to pull out a seat.

'We've been a little worried about you lately. We haven't been seeing you in church so often these days. I do hope it's nothing to do with your health.'

'Nae in as mony words,' said Babbie.

A waitress came and offered Mr Thole a menu, but he declined and said he was only visiting. The waitress did not look best pleased and left.

'It's just that you are such an assiduous churchgoer that we wondered if you needed any help or anything. Transport perhaps?'

'Thank ye, Mr Thole,' said Babbie, 'bit, no. I'll manage a Sunday walk tae the kirk, decrepit as I am. I've jist hid one or two ither things on ma plate, lately. I hope ye dinna mind.'

'Not a bit. Not a bit. We were just concerned for you.'

There was an awkward silence for a moment as Babbie wondered if she should explain that she had an appointment and she had no time for social pleasantries, even from the minister. Mr Thole, meanwhile, was simply wondering if there was anything more to say.

'Ye're surely affa worried aboot yer congregation drappin aff,' said Babbie. 'Still lookin gey thin in the pews, is't?'

Mr Thole was mildly taken aback at so direct a question. 'It *is* looking a little thin, as a matter of fact. No matter what I try, I can't seem to persuade people that a Sunday visit to church is the right thing to do.'

Babbie looked at her watch and then at the clock, but Mr Thole was off on a different train of thought and did not take the hint.

'I mean,' he said, 'it's not as if the Church is thoroughly irrelevant these days. Heavens, we need simply read our newspapers and watch our televisions to witness all the dreadful things that are happening in the world and we simply know how relevant the Church is even now.'

He looked up. 'Don't you agree?'

'Fairly,' said Babbie. She shoved her seat back from the table, hoping that that would do the trick.

'Perhaps if we could work out some practical way of becoming involved in people's lives, rather than just expecting them to be the ones to be involved actively by visiting church on a Sunday – perhaps that would be the answer, do you think?'

'I'm nae really the richt person tae ask, Mr Thole,' said Babbie. She looked at her watch again.

'Oh, am I holding you back?'he said at last.

'Not at all. Not at all,' said Babbie, but she stood up, anyway. 'I've a twa–three thingies needin deein at hame, so I'll say cheerio aenoo and I hope ye get yer problem sortit oot wi yersel.'

'Do you think society's morals have degenerated too far for me to have any effect?' said Mr Thole. He stood up, too.

'I beg yer pardon?'

'Do you think I'm too late? Do you think, you know, that people are too concerned with the pleasures of the flesh to be concerned with the pleasures of the spirit?'

'I couldna really say. I'm a pensioner.'

'I sometimes worry about how lightly the young people of today respect themselves, you see,' said Mr Thole. 'The problem is that they appear to have little or no self-respect. Moral education, I think, is overdue. Don't you? Are you disappointed by how readily people surrender to impulses?'

'Mr Thole, I'll hae til awa. I'll think aboot it and let ye ken.'

'Perhaps I could visit and we could discuss it some time.'

'Gie's a phonie first, though. Cheerio.'

THE plumber and the sparky were waiting patiently outside Babbie's gate by the time she bustled up.

'Affa sorry,' she gasped. 'Affa sorry. I wis held up wi the minister newsin aboot sex.' The tradesmen looked at each other. 'Come awa in.'

For most of that morning, the tradesmen clattered and hammered and clanked with pipes and tiles, battens and hammers. As expected, Virginia and Erchie found reason to visit and professed surprise at how radical an overhaul Babbie was contemplating.

They had gone home when one of the tradesmen appeared at the kitchen door.

'Mrs Girn,' he said. 'I'll need yer advice here. The shower tray fits fine, and there's nae trouble wi the plumbin or nithing, bit we'll need tae ken fitna waa o the shower ye're needin yer seat installed.'

Babbie wiped her hands on a towel and followed the tradesman up to the bathroom.

'Oh, that's a fine big shower tray,' she said. 'I'll get easy moved aboot in that.'

She stepped inside and played out the actions of standing up and sitting down on an imaginary seat attached to each of three walls.

'I'm nae affa sure,' she said. 'Fit's yer advice?'

The plumber climbed in. 'If ye pit it on that wa,' he said, 'I'll need tae tak a pipe roon an extra twa fit or so. If ye pit it . . .'

The phone began ringing.

'Dash it,' said Babbie. 'I'd better get that.' She clambered past the plumber and trotted downstairs.

'Hello? Oh, Mr Thole, it's yersel.'

'Hello, Mrs Girn. I do apologise for my despondency earlier on today, but you lifted my spirits.'

'Weel, that's good. Happy tae help.'

'So, I was wondering. Our little chat. When do you think we might manage that?'

'Wir chat?'

'You know, about how society's morals appear to be slipping into a morass of degradation and sleaze.'

'Oh, nae this aifterneen, onywye, Mr Thole. I'm in the shower wi the plumber.'

16 *Wartime Brasso and Carrots*

IT was a wonder the roar of derision had not been heard across half of the Vale of Stronach. At the lounge bar of the Stronach Arms, the sceptics were ranked against Gibby Spurtle as he struggled manfully to explain his theories on healthy eating.

He had explained that spinach was packed with iron and helped build muscles; that milk was strong on calcium and helped to strengthen teeth, and that six daily slices of wholemeal bread were all a body needed to keep coughs and sneezes at bay.

But when he suggested that white spots on the nails were a sign of heart disease, the interest of his audience evaporated and turned to guffaws of laughter.

'Awa ye go,' said John the Barman. 'Michty, Gibby, ye spik some affa rubbish whiles. Aul wives' tales. That's aa ye spoken the nicht. Aul wives' tales. Awa and jine the Rural.'

'Scientific fact,' said Gibby. 'They've proved it ower and ower again. It's an aa the Government health adverts and aathing.'

'Aye, weel,' said Sandy Brose. 'Will ye hae anither halfie, Doctor Spurtle?'

'Ye may mock,' said Gibby, 'bit I'm richt eneuch, and ye ken fine that I am. It's fowk lik you that's costin the National Health aa the money; aetin aa the wrang stuff, nae exercisin, puffin fags and gawpin at the TV ilky nicht. Nae muckle winner the hospitals hinna beds fin fowk lik you dinna look efter themsels.'

'Bit fite spots on yer nails,' said Walter Dreep, and the gently patronising tone in Walter's voice infuriated Gibby even more than the open mockery of the others.

'Fit ither aul wives' tales hiv ye got for's?' said Sandy. 'Dinna scale saut, for it's nae lucky? A pregnant wifie's haein a loon if she's oot at the front, and a quine if she's oot at the sides? If the nowt lie doon, it'll be rainin in the oor?'

'Please yersel,' said Gibby. 'Lach awa. Lach awa. See if I'm bathered.

I'll tell ye this, though, I'll still be trim and fit at your age, lang efter you're awa.'

'Ye'll be tellin's next that ye aet plenty carrots for they help ye see in the dark,' said John.

The hoots of laughter grew even louder.

It took Erchie Sotter to bring order into proceedings.

'And he'd be richt,' said Erchie. The assembly fell silent and looked round.

'Nae you as weel, Erchie?' said John.

'No,' said Erchie, 'nae me. An aul RAF crony o mine in the war.'

'RAF?'

'RAF.'

'I thocht you were in the Gordons in Normandy?' said John.

'And the SAS in Burma,' said Sandy.

'And the Special Operations Executive in North Africa,' said Walter.

'And I'd a twa–three month amon the RAF bombers oot o Norfolk in 1944,' said Erchie. 'That's far I met Brasso. Ronnie Brassfield wis his name – fae Kent somewye – bit we jist ca'ed him Brasso. He wis wir tail-end Charlie – the rear gunner. A richt fine boy. Affa dedicated til his post. Ye felt safe wi Brasso at yer back. The trouble wis, he'd jist this one worry. Day and nicht, he worried aboot it.'

Erchie finished the last of his half-pint and wiped the back of his hand across his lips. The five others, glasses in hand, waited for the story to continue. But Erchie appeared to have stalled.

'So?' said Sandy eventually. 'Fit wis yer man's worry?'

'Richt thirsty wark, this reminiscin,' mused Erchie.

'John, a halfie for Doctor Kildare here,' said Sandy.

'As I wis sayin,' said Erchie. 'Brasso his jist this one worry. He wis worried that his nicht vision wisna fit it micht be. As ye wid understand, nicht vision wis crucial for bomber crew durin the waar.'

'So he wis declared unfit for bomber crew?' said Sandy.

'Nivver an unfit,' said Erchie. 'Michty, there wisna that mony aircrew durin the waar that ye could throw them awa on a whim. Na, na. He went til the station MO and ye ken fit the station MO telt him?'

'Eat carrots?' offered John.

'Exactly,' said Erchie. ' "Eat carrots, Brassfield," he says. "Eat carrots and you'll have night vision like nothing on earth, I guarantee."'

'There ye go,' interrupted Gibby. 'Fit did I tell ye? If RAF doctors were spikkin sense lik that durin the war, is it nae high time the rest o ye cottoned on?'

'And did he eat carrots?' asked Walter.

'Brasso?' said Erchie. 'I'll sweir he ate carrots. Carrots for his breakfast. Carrots for his denner. Carrots for his tea. He'd carrot soup, carrot stew and carrot juice. He even took a twa–three carrots wi him on bombin runs.'

'And did it work?' said John.

'Of coorse it must hiv workit,' said Gibby triumphantly. 'It's common knowledge that carrots is packit wi Vitamin A for nicht vision.'

'Well, it did work and it didna,' said Erchie.

'It did and it didna?' said John.

'Aye,' said Erchie. 'It fairly perked up his nicht vision. Michty, he wis seein things in the dark that the rest o's couldn't mak oot ata. There wis jist ae problem.'

'And fit wis that?'

'He kept trippin ower his lugs.'

17 *Dorothy's Aches and Pains*

THE intercom buzzed in the consulting room. The doctor looked up from his notes, reached over and pushed the Talk button. 'Yes, Janice.'

'I thought you should know, doctor,' said the receptionist, 'that that's Dorothy Birze just arrived at the surgery.'

He sighed. 'All right. Thanks for the warning.'

The doctor sat for a moment and sighed again. He had not seen Dorothy for more than two years. Fellow-patients had complained of her presence and chatter in the surgery waiting-room until he had had to take her aside one difficult morning and suggest to her that he would accord her the privilege of home visits from then on.

She was supposed to have been flattered, but Dorothy had seen through the ploy at once and had been hurt deeply. As she told Babbie Girn the day after the bombshell dropped: 'I wis only newsin.'

But Dorothy had been newsin in the surgery waiting-room five days a week, and now it seemed as if the cycle was about to start again. The doctor sighed once more and wondered if he should nip it in the bud, or let it run and hope that it petered out without intervention.

Or maybe she was genuinely ill.

After three or four more patients, all with summer coughs and sniffles, he walked through to reception, picked up the file of notes handed him by Janice and poked his head into the waiting-room.

'Mrs Birze?' he said, backing out again almost at once. Dorothy picked up her handbag and trotted out behind him.

'Hello, doctor,' she said as she followed him to the consulting room. He entered, held the door open and closed it behind her. Then he walked towards his desk, looking at her notes. 'Have a seat,' he said, idly pointing at the chair beside the desk.

When he looked up a few moments later, Dorothy was lying on the couch against the far wall, staring at the ceiling.

He stood up and pulled his chair across to the side of the couch.

'We haven't seen you here for a while.'

'I ken, doctor, bit I've been affa nae weel.'

'A home visit is still perfectly all right, you know.'

'I didna like botherin ye,' she said. 'Ye maun be real busy aenoo.'

'Anyway, what's ailing you?'

'I've a bit o a sair throat,' she said. 'Ma knee's giein me gip again. I've an affa furry feelin on ma tongue ilky mornin. There's a bit rash on the back o ma haun. I've an affa tingly feelin across ma shooders and there's a buzzin in ma heid.'

'I see, well . . .'

'. . . and diarrhoea.'

'But apart from that, you're all right in yourself?'

'Smashin.'

'So where will we start? Let's see.'

'Ye dinna mind me comin back efter you bannin me fae the surgery twa year syne?'

'It was hardly a ban, Mrs Birze.'

'That's fit it felt like.'

'Well, I'm sorry about that. It wasn't intended to. We just wanted you to be attended to safely at home.'

'And I likit comin in for yer bedside manner. Ye've an affa good bedside manner, doctor. Yer bedside manner's jist special. Aabdy in the village says that.'

'That's very kind of them, I'm sure. I'll just take your pulse.'

'There's nae mony doctors wi a bedside manner lik yours. Nae muckle winner fowk likes comin in. It's better nor a wikk at Butlin's, haein a newsie wi you.'

'Really.'

'Aye, really. Better nor a holiday. Foo's ma pulse?'

'Ticking over nicely. We'll do your BP.'

'We'd a richt gweed doctor ower at Methlick, of coorse. I'd a lotta time for him. A nice, kind aul man. *He* wid often say that I wid get special treatment and he wid sign a special consent so that I wid get hame visits aa the time.'

'Is that so? A man ahead of his time, clearly.'

'And what a humour. I mind seein him because o a flutter in ma hert. And he took a bit listen and then he lookit up and he says: "Mrs Birze," he says, "yer hert'll laist as lang as ye live." Now, wisn't that witty?'

'He should have been on the stage.'

'I telt him that. 'Ye should be on the stage, doctor,' I says. 'It wis his humour that helpit fowk get better, I wyte.' She touched the doctor's knee gently. 'You've that same humour, doctor.'

The doctor shifted uneasily.

Dorothy lay back on the couch and looked at the ceiling again. 'And I mind fin ma brither wis oot in the chaumer playin the moothie ae nicht and something must hiv surprised him, I dinna ken fit. Onywye, he swallaed his moothie.'

'A whole harmonica, swallowed?'

'The hale jing-bang. Jammed in his throat. We heard it happenin, aa this wheezin and hootin, bit we jist thocht he wis playin something new-fangled. Then he cam across the close, his face lik a turkey-cock, and the noises comin oot o his throat . . . like the Barnyards o Delgaty and the National Anthem aa throwe een anither. Ilky time he hoastit, he hit Tap C.

'Onywye, ma faither hammered him on the back and we got it up, and I ran for the doctor and the doctor jist drappit fit he wis deein and gied me a lift back in his Austin Chummy and he took a look at ma brither, lyin back on the bed, and fit div ye think wis the first thing he said?'

'I can't imagine.'

'He says: 'Swallaed a moothie, Jim? Weel, look on the bricht side. Ye could hiv been playin the pianna.'

18 Erchie's Monday Blues

ERCHIE Sotter stood at his front door and surveyed the happenings in the Main Street. It was a while since he'd known a July to be so hot. The summer of '76 was the last one, as far as he recalled, when he had been a spry young thing in his mid-fifties.

Erchie stepped down on to the bottom step and the force of the sun hit him full-face. He flinched and blinked until he became accustomed to the heat then, squinting against the light took a few steps along his garden path, noticing how dry everything was and remarking that he would have to do some serious watering that night if he wasn't to lose most of his lobelia and aubretia.

He must have been staring at them a little longer than he had imagined, for he was woken from his reverie by a bright voice.

'Hello, Mr Sotter.'

Erchie looked up. There in the sunlight, wearing a light cotton frock and an extremely pretty smile, was Floretta Brose.

'Hello,' said Erchie. 'Michty, it's young Floretta.'

'Ye're sunnin yersel?' she said.

'I widna say that, lass,' said Erchie. 'I wis thinkin the grun's affa dry. We could be deein wi a suppie rain.'

'So ye'll be oot wi the roozer the nicht,' said Floretta brightly.

But Erchie didn't answer. Instead, his head dropped and he looked at his plants again.

'I'm sayin ye'll be oot wi the waterin-can,' said Floretta.

'Eh?' said Erchie. 'Oh, aye, the roozer. Richt enough. The roozer.'

Floretta stepped a little closer to the dyke. 'Mr Sotter, are ye aaricht?'

Erchie looked at her. 'Am I aaricht?' he said quietly. 'Am I aaricht? Weel, noo, that's nae easy answered. If ye mean am I still breathin, still aetin, still sleepin and still managin a halfie in the pubbie noo and again, then I suppose I'm aaricht. If ye mean, am I in the prime o life, wi plenty ti look forrit til, fowk roon aboot me and aa ma faculties still singin lik they did forty–fifty year ago, then I doot, no, I'm nae aaricht.'

'Oh, Mr Sotter,' said Floretta sadly. 'Are ye nae weel?'

Erchie smiled wanly. 'Jist ma age, lass,' he said. 'Jist ma age. There wis a whilie there I thocht I'd go on for ivver, and now I'm thinkin that I winna – and even supposin I could, I dinna think I wid hae the strength.'

Floretta said nothing, but she studied him.

'I'd a trippie til London a coupla month ago,' he said. 'Won it in a competition. Doon on an aeroplane fae Dyce and aathing. Good hotel. Rare grub. The works. And I jist thocht til masel that there's still sic a lot I hinna deen. There's fowk nooadays that think nithing o fleein half wye roon the world for a holiday. And then there's folk like me.'

'Bit what a lot ye *hiv* deen,' said Floretta. 'Aa yer heroics in the war, and yer time trainin the Gurkhas in the jungle, and capturin enemy sojers efter D Day and rescuin foreigners and aa that kinna thing.'

But Erchie just smiled. 'Aye,' he said. 'Richt enough. Erchibald Sotter VC, DSO and bar.' He looked up. 'There wis a time in my young day fan lassies wisna safe roon aboot me, ye ken. In my young day, if a lassie stoppit ootside my front gate weerin a little frockie like yours I wid hiv loupit the fence and we'd be awa for a walk airm in airm. Nae noo, though. I couldna jump nithing.'

'Mr Sotter,' said Floretta softly. 'I'm nae interferin or bein funny or onything, bit hiv ye thocht o haein a newsie wi the doctor? There's a lot they can dee nooadays.'

'New legs?' said Erchie. 'New een? New hert? New aathing?'

'Maybe no,' said Floretta. 'But he can fairly cheer ye up.'

'Dis he dee comedy turns noo, like? Peels, potions and party hats? Och, I'm sorry, lass, I ken ye mean weel, bit it's jist ma humour aenoo.'

'The change o life,' smiled Floretta.

Erchie looked at her. 'That's it,' he said, managing a wee laugh himself. 'I doot it's the change o life.'

'Well,' said Floretta, preparing to go, 'you see and look efter yersel. And mind fit I said aboot the doctor. Ye widna believe fit they can dee nooadays. And, efter aa, ye've peyed near aa yer days for a health service.'

Erchie gave her a friendly wave away and watched as she tripped brightly down the pavement, brimful of enthusiasm and cheer. Brimful of youth.

He turned and studied his garden. Then he thought for a moment.

IT was another two days before Floretta happened down the Main Street again. This time, she was wearing shorts in a fetching sky-blue shade and the weather, if anything, was even hotter. A few hundred yards ahead, she saw Erchie in his garden and wondered if she should cross the street to speak to him, or if she should stay on the opposite side of the road and pretend she had not noticed.

The decision was made for her a few moments later when Erchie stood up to take a break from his hoeing and spied her. He waved vigorously and Floretta looked both ways, crossed the street and strode up to the garden gate.

Erchie walked to his side of the gate to meet her. Even before he spoke, she could see that his humour had improved.

'Well, Mr Sotter,' she said, 'ye're lookin a bittie cheerier wi yersel the day.'

'I am that, lass. I am that,' said Erchie.

'Did ye hae a newsie wi the doctor?'

'I took yer advice, ma quine, and I jist made an appintment and I saw him last nicht. What a rare doctor we've got. He jist said that there wis plenty life left in the aul dog yet, and did I nae ken that there wis a wifie in America that didna tak up paintin picters until she wis in her eichties, and that there wis a best-sellin author in England somewye that didna write her first book til she wis aboot sivventy-nine. Weel, I'm nae eese at picters or writin, bit that's nae the pint, is it? The pint is . . . opportunities.'

'And wis that aa that he did? Jist newsed? He didna gie ye peels or onything?'

'Nivver a peel,' said Erchie. 'Although he did say that a man wi my romantic history wis likely missin female company, and hid I thocht aboot maybe takkin somebody oot for a slider some Sunday aifterneen? Then he rakit aboot in a drawer and he handed me a tape. He said I'd tae play the tape jist afore I fell asleep at nicht, and I tried it last nicht.'

'A relaxation tape?' said Floretta.

66

'I suppose it is. It's got affa queer floaty music on it. Michty, ye're awa afore ye ken ye're sleepin. The doctor said it wid help me cheer masel up in ma dreams.'

'And did ye hae dreams?'

Erchie almost blushed. 'Michty,' he said. 'Dreams? I wyte I hid dreams. What dreams I hid. I dreamed I wis sittin in a great big bubble bath wi Dolly Parton, Raquel Welch and Betty Grable. And we were aa jist sittin amon the bubbles lachin and jokin.'

'Michty, Mr Sotter,' said Floretta. 'That must hiv kittled ye up.'

'Nae as muckle as I wid hiv likit,' said Erchie. 'In ma dream, I wis Muggie Thatcher.'

19 *Gibby the Conjuror*

IT is the way of the fates that those rare moments of calm in the hurly-burly of modern existence will be shortlived, and such was the experience of Flo and Gibby Spurtle last Thursday evening.

After long and tiring days for both of them, Gibby and Flo had managed to persuade the children to bed early and were coorieing down together to watch one of the TV soaps, with a wee sweet sherry each, when there came a loud wail from upstairs. Gibby looked at Flo then slumped his shoulders. It was a slump which spoke of frustration and exhaustion and resignation.

'I'll see til her,' Flo said.

'Na, na,' Gibby said. He moved her gently to one side and laid down his glass. 'You've been on the go since six this mornin.'

'And sae hiv you,' Flo said. 'We'll baith go.'

Wayne was still sleeping the sleep of angels when his parents crept into the children's room, but Cassandra was sitting upright, gulping sobs and tears streaming down her wee round face. She made a touching, even pathetic picture, bathed in the moonlight streaming through the window.

'Now, now, now,' Gibby said, tiptoeing round the foot of Wayne's bed to get to her. 'Fit's adee here? It's come ower the TV that there's a wee lassie makkin an affa racket in a bedroom at Stronach.'

But Cassandra couldn't explain. Each time she tried, her words were lost in gulps.

Flo sat down on the edge of the bed and smoothed her daughter's hair. 'Wis it a bad dream, ma quine?' she said. Cassandra shook her head and said, between gulps: 'I'm – gaun – tae – dee.' The roaring and sobbing began anew.

Flo clutched her daughter to her chest and looked up at Gibby. It was the old nightmare about death and eternity.

'Ye're nae gaun tae dee, lass,' Flo said. 'Ye're only six. Ye've a hale lifetime o mischief in front o ye yet. Years and years and years and years.'

Cassandra pushed back and looked up at her mother. 'No,' she said. 'I – AM – gaun – tae – dee. I've swallied a penny.'

It took a few moments for the first spark of a broad grin to spread across Gibby's features, but he sat down on the bed.

'Ye've swallied a penny?' he said, and Cassandra nodded and tried wiping some of the tears from her face.

'And foo did that come aboot?'

'I wis coontin ma pennies and I swallied een,' Cassandra said.

'Well, well, well,' Gibby said. 'Ye're surely affa rich afore ye can affoord tae eat yer siller.'

Cassandra wasn't to be joked out of her despair.

'Ye ken something,' Gibby said. 'I ken a magic trick that I've been needin tae try for ages, bit it only works on specially good lassies.'

Cassandra looked at him, eyes wide in the moonlight; little body still lurching with the last remnants of a sob or two.

'Excuse me, Mrs Spurtle,' Gibby said. 'I've work tae dee.' Flo laid Cassandra back on the pillow while Gibby, covered for a moment by the change of places, dipped unseen into his pocket and palmed a penny of his own.

He sat down next to his daughter and looked at her, then closed his eyes as if concentrating hard.

'Now,' he said. 'I've tae say some magic words. Ye dinna mind if I say some magic words, div ye?'

Cassandra shook her head.

'Now,' he said, 'if only I can mind the richt words.' He made a show of trying hard to remember his magic spell. 'Eh, let me see now. Arrabadaca? No, no, it's nae that. Eh. Abbarabada? No, no, it's nae that, eether. Mercy, fit wis that magic word again?'

'Abracadabra?' Cassandra said.

Gibby snapped his fingers. 'Abracadabra. Mercy, it's richt handy haein a brainy lassie in the room. That wis the word. Abracadabra. You hinna attended the magic academy in yer spare time, hiv ye?' Cassandra shook her head.

Gibby closed his eyes again and took a deep breath. His daughter's eyes were wider than ever now. Slowly, he raised both hands, palms out, and began passing them over Cassandra's head. She tried to follow them both, certain that sparks or beams of green light were about to shower upon her. She didn't want to miss any of the spectacle.

Gibby began by humming a low note as if calling up his magic powers. He passed his hands over Cassandra a little more quickly, then stopped them over her head.

'Abracadabra,' he said quietly. He let the silence hang for a moment or two, then opened one eye. 'Onything?' he said. Cassandra shook her head. Even Flo found herself stepping to one side for a better view.

Gibby closed his eyes again, stretched out his hands a little closer to Cassandra's head this time, and said a little more loudly: 'Abracadabra.'

On the last syllable he brushed his hands lightly across her face and, in the moonlight, produced the palmed penny.

'There ye go,' he said. 'One penny oot o Cassandra's insides and ready for her purse again. Wisn't that a rare magic trick?'

Cassandra's mouth had dropped open, then she began chortling. She sat upright and peered into the palm of her father's hand, then looked up at him.

He turned round to Flo and winked and, as he did so, he felt a wee hand snatch the penny out of his palm.

He snapped round in time to see Cassandra fling the penny into her mouth and swallow hard.

'Go on,' she said, giggling with delight and clapping her hands. 'Dee't again. Dee't again.'

20 *Ghostly Encounter*

A COOL east wind was blowing over the top road on the Hill of Stronach by the time Ebenezer Grip and Erchie Sotter reached the bench at the viewpoint. Ebenezer took off his black homburg hat and dusted the wooden slats with a few quick strokes before he and Erchie eased themselves down for a rest.

'Aul age disna come itsel,' observed Erchie as, gently, he straightened a stiff leg out in front of him. 'There's times nooadays that I think I winna manage up here muckle langer.'

'Awa ye go,' said Ebenezer. 'Ye're a bairn yet compared wi me, and I'm still managin. It's only a twa–three mile. Ye're nae that decrepit yet, surely? Onywye, look at the view.'

They scanned the Vale of Stronach from north to south, saying nothing, but drinking in the sights that both had enjoyed since boyhood.

'It jist gets bonnier and bonnier, disn't it?' said Ebenezer; and Erchie smiled, for he had been thinking exactly the same thing.

'There's nae place lik hame,' said Erchie. 'There's whiles I think I hit the jackpot, bidin aa ma days at Stronach. I couldna hiv wished for better.'

They gazed out over the vale for a few moments more, watching as the sun brushed in waves along the parks of barley and as clouds scudded past the top pastures on the other side, at Bogensharn. They followed the embankments and cuttings of the old railway, silent for more than thirty years, and looked at the Water of Stronach, sparkling in July sunshine.

It was Ebenezer whose gaze first alighted on the ruined shell of the old House of Stronach, the mansion home of the Stronach family that had been consumed by fire one winter's night in the early 1950s.

'I often think fit a waste that is,' said Ebenezer.

'Fit's that?'

'The big hoose. I often think it could be taen in haun.'

'It's a ruin,' said Erchie. 'Ye'd nivver get onybody willin ti spen aa that siller restorin a ruin.'

'Bit mind foo it lookit in its glory days atween the wars,' mused Ebenezer. 'Aa the toffs and bigwigs comin up fae London and Edinburgh for their funcy pairties wi Lord and Lady Stronach. Mind foo us loons wid hide in the roddies and look at the dukes and the ladies in aa their finery, and foo the licht wid spill oot o the big windaes, wi the orchestra playin inside, and them birlin roon duncin.'

'And we nivver thocht onything o't,' said Erchie. 'We nivver thocht we wis ill-pairtit. That wis jist the wye the big fowk behaved. We jist behaved oor wye, and that wis that. Nivver nae jealousy nor nithing.'

'Aye,' said Ebenezer, 'we fairly lost something the nicht o the big fire. The vale hisna been the same since. I often think that some big company could come in and restore it and maybe mak it a posh hotel or a conference centre or something lik that.'

'Wi it haunted?' said Erchie.

'Awa ye go, haunted,' said Ebenezer. 'Flech wi yer haunted. That's a story put roon by fowk that disna ken nae better. There's nae sic thing as ghosts. Even if there wis, it wid draw fowk richt, left and centre.'

'Oh, there's fairly ghosts in the big hoose,' said Erchie. 'I ken because I saw een.'

Ebenezer took off his hat and grinned, waiting for a punchline.

'I'm nae pullin yer leg,' said Erchie. 'I saw a ghost ae nicht ten– twelve year ago fin I wis walkin roon the ruins.'

'Did it scare ye?' grinned Ebenezer.

'Nivver a scare,' said Erchie. 'I wis stannin in fit's left o the ballroom fin something made me turn roon. Up against far the big fireplace must hiv been, there wis this shimmerin kinna fite licht. I thocht it wis maybe a mark on ma glesses, so I took them aff and gied them a dicht and put them back on. Lord, it wisna a mark ata, for fin I put them back on it wis as plain as onything that it wis a ghost.'

'Weerin a sheet wi twa holes for een, I suppose.'

'Nivver a sheet. He wis weerin aul-farrant claes, richt enough, and he wis jist lookin back at me. There wis nithing til him; I could hiv walkit up til him and put ma haun richt through him. It wis jist lik a wee bittie fog.'

'Aye, in yer heid, a wee bittie fog.'

'Then he spoke,' said Erchie.

'This gets waur and waur.'

'He spoke. He said he wis the third Baron Stronach. Him that wis killed in his bed by his wife because she'd taen up wi a nobleman fae Doon Sooth.'

'So you spoke til him, I suppose.'

'I did that. In fact, we'd a richt news.'

'You and the ghost?'

'A richt news, we hid. He said he often hung aboot the hoose at nicht, despairin aboot the fire and foo centuries o tradition hid jist gaen up in flames. He said he couldna weer the thocht o some ither femly bidin there, and if Lord Jolyon didna come back fae London seen and rebuild it, he wid dee his utmost tae scare onybody else fae the place.'

'Ye tell some richt stories, Erchie,' said Ebenezer, turning to gaze at the view again.

'Nivver a story,' said Erchie. 'I telt the Baron that naebody wid believe me and I asked him if it wid be OK if I took his photie.'

Ebenezer roared with laughter and slapped his homburg off his knee. 'Let me guess, the ghost said No.'

'Believe it or no, he agreed.'

'So ye took his photie?'

'I did that. He stood in front o far the fireplace hid been and he posed, and I took oot ma camera and, FLASH, that wis that.'

'So far's the photie? How come we've nivver seen it?'

'Aweel,' said Erchie. 'It didna come oot, ye see.'

'It didna come oot. What a surprise.'

'It wis jist mair or less black. I speired at the chemist if he could try again, bit he said it wis a fault in the takkin o the picture. He said the flash surely hidna been strong enough.'

'A peety that,' said Ebenezer. 'And affa convenient if ye dinna mind me sayin. Efter you gettin a ghost tae agree tae get his photie taen, yer flash didna work richt.'

'Aye,' grinned Erchie. 'I suppose ye could say the spirit wis willin, bit the flash wis weak.'

21 *Sammy Wants a Reference*

SAMMY Dreep looked up from the kitchen table. 'It says here that I need a referee,' he announced to his parents. Walter hardly looked up from doing the dishes. 'Ye can manage findin yersel a referee surely,' he said. 'Ye've twa degrees already, and they're nae askin muckle if they're askin for a referee.'

'Fa will I get?' said Sammy.

'Laddie,' said Walter, 'if ye canna think fa'll pit in a gweed wird for ye, ye hinna muckle hope landin anither twa year at the varsity.'

'Could ye nae pit doon some o yer aul university teachers?' said Aggie. 'Wid they nae something nice aboot ye?'

'I dinna think so,' said Sammy, chewing his lip. 'Nae efter fit happened til their cars.'

'No,' said Walter. 'That wisna an affa happy episode. Still, look on the bricht side; maist o them wis jist kept in the hospital ae nicht.'

'I dinna think it wis the hospital that rattled them,' said Aggie. 'I think it wis Sammy panickin and missin his gears and reversin back ower three o them lyin in the car park. No, maybe yer university teachers is nae sic a hot idea. Fit aboot somebody in the village? Fa are we on friendly terms wi that's important? Fa div we ken that's got standin in the community?'

Walter paused in mid swirl of his dishmop and gazed blankly through the kitchen window. Aggie folded her *Press and Journal* into her lap and stared at the top of the table, deep in thought. Even Sammy put down his pen and screwed up his features to help his concentration. They stayed that way for fully a minute.

'Well, nivver mind; there's maybe somebody in The Toon,' said Walter at last. 'Fit aboot yer dentist?'

'I dinna think that coonts,' said Sammy.

'Nae efter ye took yon cramp and knocked his syringe intil his leg,' said Aggie. 'I ken he looked affa fine and peaceful lyin on the surgery fleer, bit that wisna the pint.'

74

'Fit aboot Mr Thole the meenister?' said Walter. 'He's an affa fine mannie. Mr Thole's that fine a mannie that he nearly maks me wish I went til the kirk.'

'I dinna think Mr Thole wid write me a reference,' said Sammy. 'He hisna seen me since Sunday School near fifteen year ago. Wid he nae need tae be a bittie mair up tae date wi me nor that?'

'Meenisters is meenisters,' said Walter. 'They'll dee onything if they think there's a sniff o a new recruit. Div they nae dee funerals for fowk that's nivver looked the road o them for sivventy year? That's real Christianity. That's turnin the ither chikk. That's pittin yer fellow man afore yersel. Awa doon til the kirk hall and chum Mr Thole and see fit he says. I bet he'll dee't.'

'Except . . .' said Aggie. 'I believe he's already turned doon Gibby Spurtle for a reference for a gairdener's job in The Toon, on the strength o Gibby nae attendin the kirk regular.'

'He's affa picky, that Thole mannie,' said Walter. 'Nivver likit him. Nae really.'

'The doctor,' said Sammy brightly. 'He dis references. He signed the back o ma passport photies fower year ago.'

'And we gie him plenty trade,' said Aggie, equally enthused. 'There's hardly a wikk passes that there's nae een o's doon at him. Fowk lik us keeps fowk lik him in his job. That's surely worth scrattin wir backs, wid ye nae think?'

'Weeeeel,' said Walter. 'I think doctors charges for stuff lik that nooadays. Did he nae turn himsel private a twa–three year back? Dis he nae rin the place like a business? Fit is't they ca't – fundholders? I think he his tae accoont for ivry last penny and ivry last minute o his time.'

'Och, foo muckle ink wid he use on a twa–three lines on the loon's form?' said Aggie.

'Thirty poun easy,' said Walter. 'Did he nae charge Bogies a hunder and ten poun for a medical for his insurance?'

'Bogies is a big mannie, though,' said Aggie.

'He's still nae a hunder and ten poun's worth,' said Walter. 'A hunder and ten poun and the doctor nivver even warmed his hands.'

'This still disna get me ony farrer doon the road,' interrupted Sammy. 'The deadline for this application's first post on Monday. If I dinna get it awa by teatime, I winna be studyin nae Communications Studies next term; I'll be stuck in this hoose for anither year.'

Walter and Aggie looked at each other.

'Ebenezer,' they said together.

THERE was a short queue of customers at the Emporium when Sammy arrived. He hovered at the door for two or three seconds, wondering if he should risk the shop being empty later, or if he should join the queue and hope that no one else arrived afterwards to overhear his private business.

He must have hovered a little too long, for Ebenezer looked over Dorothy Birze's shoulder. 'Hie, young Dreep. Wis ye brocht up in a barn? Shut that door afore we aa freeze.'

Sammy stepped inside and shut the door quickly. He smiled wanly at the two women in front of him.

It took fully five minutes of chatter about the weather, wins at the Inverspaver Bingo and how Tony Blair's new haircut had made him look uncannily like a toilet brush with teeth, before Sammy was left alone with his former boss.

'I wis winderin,' said Sammy. 'That is, I wis hopin. Ye micht even say, I wis kinna thinkin that . . .'

'Oot wi't. Oot wi't,' said Ebenezer. 'I hinna aa day.'

'I'm needin a favour.'

'I dinna need a message-loon,' said Ebenezer. 'I hinna hid a message-loon for near ten year noo. Nae since . . .'

'Nae since me,' said Sammy.

'You? Oh, aye, it wis you. Ye fair put me clean aff haein staff.'

'I wisna that bad,' said Sammy, staring glumly at his feet.

'Wisna that bad? Wisna that bad? Foo mony bikes did ye get through?'

'Twa.'

'It wis fower,' said Ebenezer. 'Fower bikes.'

'Three wis pinched,' said Sammy.

'And ae bike wisna. Fit happened til it again?'

'The road-roller,' mumbled Sammy.

'The road-roller,' said Ebenezer. 'Exactly.'

'So I canna ask a favour?' said Sammy, looking up.

'Speir awa, ' said Ebenezer.

'I wis kinna hopin ye wid gie me a reference. Seein as ye're a figure o standin in the community.'

'A reference,' mused Ebenezer. 'A reference. Aye, I'm a figure o standin, richt enough. Weel, OK.'

'Ye will?' Sammy could scarcely believe his luck. 'Ye'll gie me a reference?'

'Certainly I will.' Ebenezer reached for a pen. 'Although ye'd be better aff athoot it.'

22 Erchie's Mountain Rescue

THE news that a hillwalker had gone missing on the Inverspaver Way caused very little excitement either at Stronach or Inverspaver. The weather had been fine, apart from a little low mist over the Hill of Stronach, and it was hardly a 100-mile trek filled with mountain peril.

As the sergeant at the Inverspaver police station had told the hillwalkers' group leader: 'He winna hae got far because there's nae really onywye for him tae go.'

'But it's such a warren of little paths all over the place up at the top of the hill,' said the group leader, 'and it was foggy, and he must have gone off to take a picture or something, and our coach has to leave in an hour at the latest if we are to be back at work tomorrow.'

'Calm yersel, sir. Calm yersel,' said the sergeant with that monotone of someone has seen it all before.

'What about Mountain Rescue?' said the group leader brightly.

'Nae hereaboots, sir. We've a pucklie hills, nae mountains. Bein honest wi ye, there's naebody roon here gypit enough tae get lost on the Hill o Stronach.'

'Are you saying we're irresponsible?'

'Not at all, sir, though ye said yersel he wis takkin a photie.'

'And what of it?'

'Jist that there's nae mony folk taks a photie in fog. Nae folk that I ken, onywye. Maybe you use different cameras far you come fae.' The sergeant looked over the station counter at the hillwalkers' leader in his bright-yellow cagoule, his vivid-red bobble hat, his lime-green leggings and sky-blue hiking boots. 'Is he got up like yersel?'

'I beg your pardon?'

'Is he kitted oot fae the same Christmas tree as you?'

'If you mean is he equipped to the required standard of our association, then, yes, he most certainly is.'

'Then we needna worry wirsels,' said the sergeant, sitting back on his stool. 'They'll likely pick up a sightin o him real quick.'

'A passing farmer or something?'

'The space station.'

The hillwalkers' group leader was about to demand the sergeant's name and number when the station door opened and in came a similarly vivid middle-aged woman.

'Percival,' she said. 'The coach driver is getting most anxious to be off. He says we can't afford to wait, and that his overtime will cost us at least a couple of hundred pounds if we don't leave in the next five minutes.

'But Jolyon's still missing,' said Percival.

'Jolyon'll be aaricht, sir,' said the sergeant. 'Somebody'll track him doon in an oor – twa oors, tops – and we'll pit him on the train or the bus til The Toon. Then he can get a train Doon Sooth and if he's late for his work it's his ain lookoot.'

'I must say I find your manner quite offhand, sergeant.'

'Aye, weel, it's been a lang shift and I've a sair heid. Trust me, sir. He'll be found safe and weel afore lang. We hinna lost a hiker yet. In fact, somebody's maybe even trackit him doon aenoo.'

THE sergeant was correct. Erchie Sotter had trailed the party at a respectful distance, mostly because, as he had watched them in the centre of Stronach, even before they had set off, he had been alarmed by their inability to read their multitude of maps to find their way out of the village square. When he had spotted Jolyon veering off on a path to the left, he had decided to hang back and follow the straggler, just in case. Within five minutes, Jolyon had lost himself in the fog.

Erchie had watched him heading down the path to the Potch of Bogensharn and knew that he would be back very quickly, so Erchie had plunkit himself on a granite stone by the fork in the path and had taken out his pipe.

Six minutes later, Jolyon, whose trousers were now wringing and stinking up to the knees, stumbled back into view from the mist.

'Mochie day,' said Erchie.

'Thank heavens for another human being,' said Jolyon. 'I appear to be lost.'

'Is that so?' said Erchie, puffing on his pipe.

'Yes, actually,' said Jolyon. 'I appear to have become separated from my party about an hour ago and I'm sure they'll be fretting themselves stupid.'

'Foo did ye get lost, like?' inquired Erchie.

'Heaven knows,' said Jolyon, shrugging in embarrassment. 'A combination of several things. The fog. My interest in photographing rare wildflowers. The fact that the others press on without savouring the joys of the countryside. And, well, here I am.'

'Sae ye are,' said Erchie.

'So,' said Jolyon.

'So,' said Erchie.

'Well, which is the way to Inverspaver?'

Erchie lifted an arm and pointed in front of him. 'Doon by there,' he said.

'Thanks awfully,' said Jolyon. 'Thanks awfully.' And he made to go.

'Or,' said Erchie, looking round and pointing behind him, 'is it ower by there?'

Jolyon stopped. 'Don't you know?'

'It's affa foggy,' said Erchie. 'And I'm affa dry. Ye hinna a hipflask on ye?'

'I'm TT,' said Jolyon.

'TT,' said Erchie disapprovingly. 'I'm on the side o a hill in a thick fog wi an English hillwalker and he's TT.'

'Couldn't you guide me down the hill?' said Jolyon. 'You must know all these paths like the back of your hand.'

'Well, ye're richt there,' said Erchie. 'Fit I dinna ken aboot the Hill o Stronach isna worth kennin. Ye'd be in safe hands, richt enough.'

'So you'll do it? That's marvellous.'

'Ach, I canna be bothered,' said Erchie. 'I'm nae in the humour.'

'Not in the humour?' said Jolyon, blinking behind his wire-rimmed glasses and clutching the toggles on his cagoule a little more tightly.

'Nae in the humour,' said Erchie. 'I tak notions like that noo and again if I dinna feel inspired.'

'I'm lost and my colleagues will be frantic and my family will be frantic and it's . . .' He buried his head in his hands in despair.

'Div ye nae think ye're a bittie ill-prepared for a walk lik this?' said Erchie.

'What?' said Jolyon, looking up. 'Just because I don't carry booze?'

'No,' said Erchie. 'Ye hinna a map. Ye hinna decent claes. Ye hinna the wit tae stick wi ither fowk. Ye hinna nithing bit a funcie camera.'

'Now, look here,' said Jolyon. 'I'm a member of one of the prime hillwalking clubs of North-west England. We win trophies. We've featured in the Sunday supplements. I come up here to your piddling little hill, that doesn't even have any decent signs, and you think you can lecture me?'

'Bit I'm nae lost,' said Erchie.

Jolyon sighed and pushed his hand through his hair. 'Look, if I give you a tenner, you can buy yourself a few whiskies at the bar for all of next week if you like.'

'Now ye're makkin sense,' said Erchie.

'So is that agreed?' said Jolyon, fumbling in his pocket.

Erchie tilted his head skywards and felt the first blusters of wind that, he knew, would clear the fog within fifteen minutes.

'Ye could mak it twinty and I could hae a bottle and then I'd show ye a shortcut,' he said.

'Done,' agreed Jolyon, still fumbling. Erchie watched him fumble through more than a dozen zippered pockets and a dozen studded pockets before he had to confess that he must have dropped his money somewhere.

'But I can give you an IOU,' said Jolyon, as Erchie stood up.

Erchie said nothing, but merely turned and began walking back up the path.

'An IOU,' wailed Jolyon. 'What do you say?'

'Weel,' said Erchie, 'I'd say ye're still lost.'

23 *Sammy Riles Aggie*

SAMMY Dreep flicked over another page of his computer magazine and sighed a sigh of such profound boredom that his mother and father looked up. His father, Walter, smiled then carried on reading his *Press and Journal*, but a dark look flashed across his mother's jowly visage.

She shook her copy of *Home Baker's Monthly* with what she imagined was suitable displeasure and glowered at him; then she, too, returned to her reading.

All might have been well had not Sammy sighed just as profoundly at the turn of his next page. Walter looked up, but Aggie flung her magazine on to the sofa cushion beside her and stared at her son.

'And fit's adee wi you?' she demanded. 'Ye're sittin there makkin noises lik a chokit Hoover.'

'Nithing adee,' said Sammy, genuinely surprised. 'I'm jist readin ma magazine.'

'Ye're makkin an affa noise aboot it. Sighin and aathing.'

'I'm bored stiff.'

'Ye're bored stiff. Nae again. Ye're bored stiff. We've hid this discussion hunders o times afore. If ye're bored stiff get aff yer backside and get yersel a job.'

'It's nae that easy gettin a job nooadays, petal,' offered Walter, the voice of peace.

'Nonsense,' said Aggie. 'Look at yer paper. The *P and J*'s fulla jobs ilky Friday. Jobs for the chairmen o great big companies and jobs for office quines and apprenticeships. I canna understand this whinin and bleatin that goes on aboot unemployment. There's nae sic thing for folk that'll get aff their backsides instead o wallowin in their laziness and haudin oot their haun for ither folk's handoots. There's nae excuse for unemployment nooadays. Especially up here. The Scottish economy's boomin. The prime minister said so.'

'Did ye say boomin or bombin?' inquired Sammy.

'Dinna be smart wi me young man. Look at ye. Ye're nae feel; ye've a degree and the like. Mighty, there's folk withoot a sniff o a varsity – they can hardly spell or coont – and they're still makkin millions ilky month, sittin at the tap o great big companies they startit themsels wi nithing bit barefaced chikk and a ten-bob note. And you're here mollochin aboot reading magazines.

'Sae are you.'

'That's nae the same difference. You're young. Ye've yer hale life in front o ye. Mighty, there's unexplored horizons that hinna even been explored yet. There's opportuinities oot there jist waitin for somebody tae grab them by the scruff o the throat. Awa and dee some grabbin, Sammy. Awa and mak yer ain luck. Awa and pit some sweat and effort intil yer future instead o sittin here thinkin that it's pintless. There's nae nithing pintless if the result's fit ye seek. It's your future; mak something o't.'

'That's easy said.'

'It's easy deen,' countered Aggie. 'For a start, hiv ye taen a look at yersel in a mirror lately. Awa oot tae the hallstand and ask yersel: if you were a boss, wid you tak on that? I'm sure I widna. Get yersel a haircut and some richt claes, for a start.'

'Fit wye?'

'Because,' sighed Aggie, 'if ye get yersel a good haircut and some presentable claes, ye've won half the battle. There wis an article in the *Press and Journal* nae twa wikks syne aboot how presentation wis eichty per cent o gettin a job at an interview. It's nae fit ye ken, it's the wye ye present yersel. And I quite believe it. It stands tae reason. Folk that smartens themsels up get ahead o the crowd fin there's jobs on the go.'

'Fit wye?'

'For the very simple reason that if ye land a job, they pey ye siller. Siller. Ye ken. The stuff me and yer faither doles oot tae keep ye. The stuff we should hiv been usin for wir retirement, bit we're spennin keepin you in the style that ye've slumpit intil. The stuff that aabody needs if they're tae mak onything o themsels. The stuff that maks the world turn. The stuff you hinna got, but fit ye'd hae if ye got yersel a job.'

'Fit wye?'

Aggie glared at her husband, as if Sammy's reluctance to follow her logic had been somehow passed down to their son from Walter's side of the family.

'Because,' she began patiently, 'wi siller, ye spend a bittie and ye save a bittie. And if ye save a bittie, ye've aye got a little nestegg for faain back on. Ye've aye got a little something for a rainy day, so fin the bad times hit, ye're nae flattened aathegither. Ye've got reserves ye can rely on. Ye're nae dependent on ither folk. Ye've taen responsibility for yersel. Ye've planned yer savins. Savins is the secret nooadays.'

'Fit wye?'

Aggie stood up.

'Because,' she said, scarcely controlling herself, 'if ye save enough money, or invest enough money, ye can mak even mair money and that'll be even better for ye.'

'Fit wye?'

'Because if ye build up a big enough nestegg wi aa this workin and savin and investin and dividends that ye're sittin on the tap o, there'll come a time fin ye've made that muckle siller that ye can retire young and nivver need tae work again.'

'Bit I'm nae workin noo.'

24 *Mother Dreep Takes a Dwaum*

JOHN the Barman and Erchie Sotter looked up as the double doors of the Stronach Arms lounge opened and chill October blew in. 'Sandy,' said both by way of acknowledgement as Sandy Brose strode in. 'An affa nicht o caul.'

Sandy hauled off his jacket and hung it open before rubbing his hands together and strolling across to the bar.

'Nae oppo the nicht?' inquired Erchie. 'Is Wattie held back deein the ironin?'

Sandy shook his head gravely. 'Na,' he said. 'A lot waur nor that. His mither's nae jaikin weel ata. xxShe took a turnie this aifterneen. The doctor's been there aa day near. He says she'd hae a better chunce if she wis moved intil Foresterhill, bit he's nae sure she wid laist the distance, so they're jist watchin her close and keepin her at hame.'

Erchie sucked gravely on his pipe. 'I dinna like hearin news lik that,' he said. 'Peer aul wifie. Will she recover?'

Sandy shrugged his shoulders. 'Fa kens?' he said. 'She's ninety-twa. She's hid a fair innins. Bit it canna hae been muckle o a life for her this list fower–five year since she moved in wi Wattie and Aggie. Could ony o us thole lyin wirsels daily-day in a bed in the front room, starin at fower waas, gettin yer maet on a tray?'

The silence was ample evidence that none of the three could contemplate such an existence.

'Is there onything we can dee?' said John. 'Flooers or something? Chocolates? A cardie?'

Sandy shook his head. 'John, I couldna tell ye. I dinna think she wid ken the difference, fae fit Wattie says. I suppose ye could send a Get Well cardie bit, ye ken fit like, as sure's fate ye'll jist hae postit the cardie and she breathes her last, and then ye've the embarrassment o wishin her weel and her lyin caul in the front bedroom. It's affa difficult, isn't it?'

'Weel,' said Erchie, stretching as he sat upright. 'I some doot I'll be lookin oot the funeral suit afore lang.'

John and Sandy looked at him, aghast at his lack of sensitivity.

'There's nae pint shilly-shallyin aboot it,' said, catching their wounded looks. 'It comes til's aa, and though I widna wish the wifie ony ill, ye maun see fit's fit. Dinna tell me it hisna been gaun through the minds o Wattie, Aggie and their loon. Tak it fae a mannie that kens, that's fit they'll be thinkin aboot.'

'Surely no,' said John.

'If they're sensible, they will be,' said Erchie. 'Ye maun be prepared for ilky eventuality. If ye're prepared, it's a lot less hard on yersel.'

'Bit fit preparin is there in a funeral at Stronach?' said John. 'Ye jist phone up Timmer Jake. He comes by wi his tape measure, phones the daily paper, and three days later it's aa feenished and ye're back in yer hoose nae kennin fit's happened. That's the pint aboot funerals. Aabody else dis the work because ye're nae fit yersel.'

'I still say preparation's the secret,' said Erchie. 'There wis a big story in the *Press and Journal* the ither day aboot foo the sensible fowk comes tae terms wi a death in the faimly, and they discuss it and they plan for't and they're nae feart o't. And if it's in the *Press and Journal*, it'll be richt eneuch.'

There was another silence as the three of them contemplated the nature of life, death and the mysterious cycle of creation.

John shoved a half pint of lager towards Sandy, and Sandy shoved a pile of change towards John. The ritual had not changed in almost twenty years, but a Thursday night without Walter Dreep by his side lent it a faintly surreal air, and gave Sandy an uneasy feeling about mortality.

'It maks ye shiver, disn't it?' he said.

'Fit, nae haein a drink?' said Erchie.

Sandy fumbled in his pocket for more change and nodded to John, who poured a small whisky and slid it over to Erchie.

'No,' said Sandy. 'Death comin sae close. I could near feel it in the caul air as I wis walkin doon here the nicht. It's an affa thing, richt enough. I mean, here I am near sixty. There you are, Erchie; you're nearer eichty than sivventy. Fin ye think aboot it, we're nae that far ahen the aul wifie. It winna be lang afore it's oor shottie. We're weerin closer.'

Erchie shot an alarmed look at John, then turned to Sandy. 'Michty, loon, ye're affa depressin company the nicht. I ken it's sad and things is nae lookin affa rosy for the aul wifie, bit life goes on.'

'That's the pint,' said Sandy. 'It disna.'

'I mean, there's nithing ye can dee aboot it,' said Erchie. He paused for a moment. 'Will we drink a toast til her?'

Sandy raised his glass weakly, and John and Erchie followed suit. 'Beldie Dreep,' they said. 'God preserve her.'

'Hiv ye ivver thocht,' said Erchie, trying to change the subject slightly, 'foo ye wid like ti go yersel?'

'Mak it quick,' said Sandy. 'I couldna thole hingin aboot waitin.'

'No, I mean, foo wid ye like tae be remembered? Fit wid ye wint for yer funeral?'

'Now fa's bein depressin?' said Sandy.

'It's nae depressin,' said Erchie. 'I often tak a bit lach til masel at nicht thinkin aboot ma ain beerial and fit fowk'll be deein and fit they'll be sayin aboot me.'

'And fit conclusions hiv ye come til, like, Erchie?' said John.

'Nae fuss,' said Erchie. 'Nae greetin. Nae wailin and singin and the organ aff-key at the kirk. Mak it simple and straightforward. Dinna ging intil a lang lingie aboot ma war heroics for ye'll be there aa day. Na, get me pluntit quick, tell a puckle stories amon yersels and . . .' Erchie almost giggled, '. . . and ye ken the best bit?'

'No, fit's the best bit?'

'I wint the men that tak a cord tae wrax intil their jaicket pooches and tak oot a half-bottle o whisky each. I wint them tae screw aff the cappies and I wint them . . .'

He paused for dramatic effect.

'. . . I wint them tae pour the hale lot ower ma grave. A last damnt gweed dram for masel at some ither body's expinse.'

John and Sandy looked at each other.

'An affa waste o gweed whisky that, Erchie,' observed Sandy.

Erchie shrugged as if to indicate that he couldn't help that, for it was his last request.

'I'll tell ye fit,' said Sandy, smiling at last. 'Could we nae gie the whisky a bit sweel roon wir kidneys first?'

25 Peaceful End for Mother Dreep

NEWS of Mother Dreep's death spread quickly and quietly round the Vale. It was discussed in hushed tones as people were out doing their Saturday-morning messages. It was whispered neighbour to neighbour. Down at the hotel, it was the only topic of conversation among farm-workers who had come into the village for their customary stovies and oatcakes.

'Jist wore awa, I suppose,' said Bogies, voicing the feelings of most of his fellow-diners as he horsed into a bowl of broth. 'A gweed innins, like. Ninety-two? Ye canna complain aboot 'at. Nae ninety-two. Man, if she'd held on a whilie langer, she micht hiv made the telegram.'

'Nae telegram noo,' said Gibby Spurtle. 'Jist a bittie in the paper.' He handed a copy of the *Press and Journal* to Bogies, who turned to page three, cleared his throat and began reading

> Stronach's oldest resident, Mrs Isabella Dreep, has died at her home in the village. She wis ninety-six.

He looked up. 'Ninety-six. Michty, I didna think she wis aa that.' He shook the paper and went back to reading.

> A former president of Stronach WRI, Mrs Dreep was born at Memsie, near Fraserburgh, and spent most of her life as a farm-worker's wife, first at Memsie and later moving to the farm of Wester Bogensharn, Stronach. After being widowed, she moved to stay with her son, Walter, and daughter-in-law and grandson in the village.

Bogies stopped reading. 'And that's it,' he said. 'Feenish't. Nae muckle for ninety-six year, is't? Twa–three lines and that's her forgotten. She'll be rowin up a fish supper the morn. Man, it gie's ye a shak fin ye see't in black and fite!'

'Fit wye dis the papers nae tell the full story?' said Gibby. 'I'm sure if they kent foo muckle a body hid achieved, they micht gie them a bittie mair space nor jist a twa–three lines. Fit wye div they nae tell foo she coped wi a man that couldna stick at onything? Fit wye div they nae tell that she did mair fairm work than he ivver did? Fit wye div they nae tell foo she tholed his philanderin? Fit wye div they nae say that she tholed his Holy Wullieness, even though he wis aye aff wi ither weemin?'

'Aye,' said Bogies. 'Queer that. I mind the time I wis roon by the cottar hoosie fin he come hame bleezin. He'd the stink o perfume aa ower him and he wis roarin lines fae the Bible.'

'Lines fae the Bible?'

'Aye, stuff like: "Jesus said go forth and multiply."'

'I bet she took him quaetly b'the haun and led him upstairs and put him til his bed til it wore aff,' said Gibby.

'Damn the linth,' said Bogies. 'She battered him roon the airse wi the fryin-pan and said that she kent fine Jesus hid said awa forth and multiply, bit that He hidna meant that it wis a job for jist ae man.'

VIRGINIA Huffie knocked briefly on Babbie Girn's back door and strode in. 'Only me,' she trilled. 'Ye'll hiv heard?'

'Aye,' said Babbie, sitting by the window. 'We're weerin closer wirsels. Ach, she wis ninety-six, and she'd nae life lyin in that bed in the front room day in, day oot. It's maybe coorse tae say, bit she's better aff up the golden staircase; awa fae'e aa.'

'That's affa genteel o ye, Babbie,' said Virginia. 'I aye thocht ye couldna thole the wifie.'

'I couldna, bit I dinna spik ill o the deid. She nivver did nithing coorse til me; I jist didna like the wye she took ower the WRI as if it wis her ain private club. Aathing we did hid tae suit her. If it didna suit her, we didna dee't. That's nae fit the WRI's aboot. Ye ken fine yersel, it got that bad that she wisna happy orderin's aboot in the hallie once a month, she thocht she could tell's foo we should rin wir private lives as weel. She wis dolin oot advice far it wisna socht. And fit aa did we nae hear aboot her treasures?'

'The box wi the valuables and the joolery,' Virginia said. 'Walter and Aggie'll be aaricht noo. The wye she spoke, it wis a fortune.'

'Maybe. Maybe no,' said Babbie. 'Walter and Aggie winna be ony better aff, though. She aye swore that it wisna tae be touched, even efter she wis deid. Div ye nae mind? She said it wis tae be kept in the laft so that it wid be easy found fin her time came and she could jist pick it up on her road til the hereaifter.'

'Noo that ye mention't, I div mind something aboot 'at.'

'Aye,' said Babbie. 'I aye thocht she'd hiv been quicker keepin't doon in the cellar.'

26 *Vale Pays Last Respects*

IT was one of those dreich October days when Stronach turned up at the cemetery to pay its last respects to Mother Dreep. More than 200 had packed the village kirk for a simple service by the Rev. Montgomery Thole, who had spoken of her strong spirit and indomitability, and her quiet final years living with her son, daughter-in-law and grandson.

The congregation was composed and reflective and filed quietly from the pews when the time came, then walked slowly behind the old Humber Pullman hearse of Timmer Jake to the small graveyard at the north end of the village.

At the graveside, Mr Thole's words seemed to carry out across the vale as he bade their sister's soul safe passage into the peace of eternity. He turned from the graveside, said a few words of comfort to Walter and Aggie, then stepped on leaving them to their thoughts and their fellows.

There was not much said. A few knowing touches on the arm was about the size of it, although one or two made innocuous comments about the weather.

As the crowds wore away towards the gate, only a few stragglers were left; the ones who knew they wouldn't be able to come back the following day to read the cards on the wreaths.

Across against the far wall of the cemetery, they might have noticed a lone figure studying proceedings. They might have seen how uneasy he appeared in an ill-fitting suit; that he was coatless despite the damp and intense cold, and how tired he was. Sammy Dreep had not slept long or well since his grandmother's death.

Erchie Sotter might not have seen him had he not stopped to read the inscription on another gravestone. When he looked up, Sammy was standing there, alone, watching his grandmother's fresh grave at thirty yards' remove.

Erchie paused for a while, then began walking towards the boy slowly. Even when he was within feet of him, Sammy neither looked up nor spoke. Erchie stopped next to him, studied him, then turned and stood himself against the wall, too.

There was a silence for fully a minute before Erchie said: 'A caul day for't.'

Sammy nodded and managed a faint: 'Aye.'

'A tyeuch aul body, laistin as lang as she did.'

'Aye.'

'Ninety-six, the paper said. Wis she aa that?'

'Ninety-six past July. We gied her a pairty.'

'She'll hiv enjoyed that.'

'Aye.'

'Are ye comin doon til the hoose oot o the caul? Yer mither'll be gled o the help, I'm sure.'

'Nae jist yet, Erchie. I'll bide a whilie, I think.'

'Ye'll ken best yersel. Affa caul, isn't it? Sna afore lang. Ye can feel it.'

'She wis as richt as rain the day it happened. It wis jist lik turnin aff a switch.'

'And that's fit wye ye maun mak the maist o fit ye've got, ma loon. Dinna waste a day o't.'

Sammy looked at Erchie. 'It's affa the wye ye learn yer lessons, isn't it?'

'As lang's ye learn them. Bit, michty, she widna hiv wintit ye catchin yer death and bein as gloomy as this. Come on awa hame. I'm needin a cuppie and a fine piece even if you're nae.' Erchie put an arm on Sammy's shoulder and propelled him forward on to the cemetery path.

'Now, tell me, fit aboot this romance we've aa been waitin for in the village? You and the lassie Brose. Nae waddin bells yet?'

'Nae waddin bells,' said Sammy. 'Aabdy's waitit a lang time for that. I doot they'll wait a lang time yet.'

'Now, mind, seize the day,' said Erchie.

'It's nae as easy as that. There's an added complication, as ye micht say. I'm seein somebody else.'

'Twa at ae time?'

Sammy nodded and Erchie beamed. 'Ye're some billie,' he said.

'It's maks life affa complicated,' said Sammy. 'Here's Floretta at Stronach and Gladys in the Toon.'

'Gladys?'

'She bides in a big hoose in the West End. She's a bittie auler nor me. Her man deed ten–twelve year ago. He wis a company boss in fish or something. She's got a Mercedes and a villa in Portugal.'

'Man, ye dinna let the grass growe. I suppose ye canna mak up yer mind atween this Gladys and wir ain Floretta?'

'Exactly. Gladys . . . well, Gladys is richt fine company and aathing, bit Floretta's mair . . . well, Floretta.'

'So fit's yer pick? That's the question.'

'That's the question, richt eneuch. Fit div ye think yersel?'

'Nae muckle o a dilemma ata, if ye ask me. Ye pick the een that yer hert tells ye.'

'Aye?'

'Ivry time. Nae question. This Gladys is maybe rollin in siller and Floretta's maybe on her last maik, bit nivver mind fit yer heid's sayin; yer hert's tellin ye truth.'

'So ye're sayin Floretta?'

'No, you're sayin Floretta. And, mind, seize the day.'

Sammy managed a faint smile. 'Ye're richt,' he said, and suddenly he seemed to walk a little more upright and a little of the cold that hung about him seemed to dissipate.

'And anither thing,' said Erchie.

'Fit?'

'Seein as ye winna need it noo, fit's Gladys's phone number?'

27 *Ambrosia Seeks Advice*

ALL the usual music of a morning fly cup halted for a moment. Babbie looked at Virginia, who just stared down at her saucer, the heat rising in her face. She had rarely been so embarrassed. Babbie turned back to her other visitor.

'Are you tellin me, Ambrosia Girn, that this baby ye're expectin is nae yer man's?'

'I canna be richt sure,' Ambrosia said. 'Bit I dinna think so.'

'And ye've come aa the wye fae Fraserburgh on three buses tae tell me this. I hope ye're nae expectin sympathy, young lady, because ye'll get nae sympathy fae me. Ye should be ashamed o yersel. Isn't that richt Virginia? Nae sympathy?'

Virginia squirmed in her seat, chewing vigorously on her ginger snap.

Babbie turned back to Ambrosia. 'Fit on earth wis gaun through that heid o yours?' she demanded. 'Hiv ye nae self-respect? Did ye nae think o yer faimly's good name at the Broch?' Babbie paused. 'Aye, weel, forget that last bit.'

Babbie reached for another butter-hard and syrup. She chewed it furiously. 'And fa's the faither?' Butter-hard crumbs sprayed across her lap.

Ambrosia shrugged and looked away.

'Ye must ken fa the faither is, surely?' Babbie said.

'I didna get a richt look at his face.'

Virginia choked on her ginger snap. She excused herself and ran to the kitchen for a gulp of water.

'Ye're a disgrace,' Babbie said. 'Ye ken that, I hope. A disgrace. I've nivver heard the like. In my day, ye'd hiv been thrown oot.'

'I could be thrown oot yet,' Ambrosia said.

'Ye hinna telt yer man yet?'

'I wis kinna hopin for advice fae you.'

'My advice, young lady, is that ye get back on the bus, get hame til

94

yer man, drap on yer knees in front o him, tell him aathing and beg for his forgiveness. If ye're lucky, he'll let ye bide, though I widna blame him supposin he flung ye oot and kickit ye twice roon the gairden. What an affront for him.'

That was when Ambrosia began to bridle. 'It's nae as black-and-fite as ye're makkin oot, Untie Babbie,' she said. 'This is nae a one-sided story, this. There's fauts on baith sides. I've lang hid my suspicions that he's been playin ahen the goal.'

She raised her hand to stop Babbie's obvious protest. 'And I ken that's nae excuse, bit it is an explanation.'

'Fit evidence hiv ye got?' Babbie said.

'Plenty evidence. Some o the fowk in the toon's telt me as muckle.'

'Steerin-up devils,' Babbie said. 'Dinna believe aathing fowk tells ye.'

'And there wis a while last year that he kept comin in late.'

'Disna mean he wis oot canoodlin. He could hiv been playin dominoes.'

'I've nivver heard it cried that afore,' Ambrosia said. 'He came in the bedroom ae nicht and he wis takkin aff his claes and he drappit his brikks and he wisna weerin ony underwear.'

'I says: "Billy," I says. "Far's yer punts?" He lookit doon and he yells: "Michty, I've been robbed."

'Now, wid you nae be suspicious?'

Babbie shifted in her seat. 'Still nae excuse,' she said. 'Twa wrangs . . .'

'. . . mak a richt soss,' Ambrosia said. 'I'm at the end o ma rope. I dinna ken far tae turn. Ma fowk hiv disowned me. Ma man'll fling me oot. Ma pals gave up on me lang ago. And now my favourite Untie Babbie's giein me a ragin. I hinna a life.'

'Dinna bother wi the saft-soap here,' Babbie said. She stood up. 'Favourite Untie Babbie, indeed. Favourite mug. I've nae siller tae gie ye.'

'I'm nae sikkin yer siller,' Ambrosia said. 'I'm needin yer moral support.'

'And I canna gie ye that, eether. So yer mission's been in vain. If the only thing ye've got against yer man is that he comes hame late some nichts, ye hinna ony cause for alarm. My hale mairriet life, yer uncle wis oot boozin at least twa–three nichts a wikk, bit ye nivver catched me gaun oot and flingin masel at the first sojer that cam roon the corner. I ken twa wrangs dinna mak a richt, bit I dinna think that fit you've been deein and fit ye think he's been deein square up ata. He's entitled tae blaa his stack wi ye, and I hope he dis exactly that, frankly. Peer mannie.'

'This wid be the same peer mannie that I spottit takkin a dame oot tae the picters in Aiberdeen jist afore Christmas,' Ambrosia said.

'I beg yer pardon?'

'I wis in the Toon deein ma Christmas shoppin ae Setterday aifterneen. I wis up at Holburn junction and ower the tops o the crowds I thocht I saw Billy, which wis queer, because he wis supposed tae be at a fitba match.

'So I chased him roon intae Holburn Street and doon tae Justice Mill Lane and I got the shock o ma life. It wis fairly Billy and it wis fairly a busty blonde that he'd got on his airm, newsin her up and lachin. They marched up the steps o the Odeon and that wis the last I saw o them. And dinna tell me she wis efter his popcorn.'

'So fit wye did ye nae follow them inside, sit doon in seats next tae them and pick the richt moment tae confront the twa o them as lang's ye'd the chunce?' Babbie said. 'Ye'd hiv hid the upper haun, then.'

'Oh, I couldna dee that,' Ambrosia said.

'Fit wye nae?'

'The boy I wis wi hid seen the fillim already.'

28 *Antiques Expert*

THE antiques expert, Jolyon Hartington-Partington, scarcely knew where to look. Even his patron, Kate Barrington-Graham, seemed surprised. It wasn't the sort of thing one expected at a summer Sunday garden party near a small Scottish village.

'Um, could you run that past me again?' said Mr Hartington-Partington.

'I'm tellin ye I ken far ye micht find the antique that ye've lookin for aa yer life,' Sandy Brose said.

'The legendary Chiagra of Kilnajar; holy grail of every antiques expert from Seattle to Sydney, from Cape Town to Caithness,' said Mr Hartington-Partington. 'The one piece of pre-Victorian cabinetmaking that outstrips even the finest Hepplewhite or Chippendale. The most exquisite piece of ebonised amboyna since . . . since . . .'

'Since ye dinna ken fan,' offered Geneva Brose.

'Mr Brose,' said Mrs Barrington-Graham, 'you'll appreciate that we find it a little hard to believe that an expert of Mr Hartington-Partington's standing has scoured the globe for years, often in the most obscure locations, hunting for the lost Chiagra of Kilnajar, and you're telling us that you know where it is.'

'I hinna telt ye that,' said Sandy. 'Aa that I've said is that I dinna seek tae raise ony spirits, bit I eence heard tell an interestin story fae an aul grieve up the glen fa's faither served in the Khyber Rifles.'

Mrs Barrington-Graham and Mr Hartington-Partington studied Sandy closely. Sandy affected a detached air, as if they could either take his story or leave it.

'Go on,' said Mr Hartington-Partington.

'Weel, ye'd better describe this bit furniture til's exackly,' said Sandy. 'I widna like tae mak a feel o masel.'

'The Chiagra of Kilnajar,' said Mr Hartington-Partington. He cleared his throat. 'Late eighteenth-century writing desk or bureau commissioned by the Sultan of Kilnajar from furniture-makers unknown, shortly before his emigration from south-eastern Asia to what is now known as India.

'Ornate and highly embellished, in ebonised amboyna. Height approximately four feet, width four feet, depth three feet. Weight unknown. Believed to have been endowed with supernatural powers. Last seen in late-Victorian London while accompanying the sultan's great-grandson on his Grand Tour of Europe in 1897. Believed to have been stolen or otherwise destroyed while on display at a gallery in New Bond Street. Estimated value on last public appearance, in excess of £230,000. Estimated value at present, if extant, beyond price.'

'That wid be aboot the size o't,' said Sandy.

'What do you mean that's about the size of it?' said Mrs Barrington-Graham.

'That's aboot the size o't. It's a gey nippy fit for the story that I wis telt fin I wis a loon.'

'Which was?'

'Ach, I dinna like tae bather onybody wi fit wis likely jist a story. Ye ken fit fowk's like roon aboot here, Mrs Barrington-Graham. Especially auler fowk. It wis likely jist a tale that grew legs and airms. Na, na, Mr Hartington-Partington, dinna ee fash yersel. Mrs Barrington-Graham's richt eneuch. Jist you cairry on lookin for yer desk lik the grand expert ye are and I'll jist cairry on fit I dee like the ignoramus I am. Now, far's the straaberry tarts?'

Mrs Barrington-Graham touched Sandy's forearm. 'Mr Brose,' she said. 'Sandy. May I call you Sandy? Sandy, at least let us hear your tale. What harm can it do? Indeed, think of all the good it could do. With the ready expertise of Mr Hartington-Partington on hand, you could be playing the key role in the discovery of the age.'

'And it wid be the discovery of the age that happened on your front green,' said Sandy.

'Heavens, I wasn't even thinking about the global interest and attendant international publicity that such an event would occasion,' said Mrs Barrington-Graham. 'Now, please, will you indulge us?'

'Ach,' said Sandy, 'it's likely jist superstitious nonsense, but nae lang efter the war, I wis sent up for a twa–three days stookin at Mains, and aul Dollop, he must hiv been near a hunder, he wid come oot wi the men at fly-time and he'd tell stories fae his faither's exploits in India lang, lang ago.

'A lotta the stories wis jist rubbish, and the men jist lached, bit there wis ae story that took me, and though I didna say nithing in front o the men for fear they micht lach at me, I collared aul Dollop efter fly-time and socht tae ken a bittie mair.

'He'd been tellin's aboot this desk that his faither hid brocht back fae India nae lang afore Queen Victoria dee't. There hid been some kinna stramash doon Bombay wye and him and a twa–three o his freens hid taen this aul desk as a kinna spoils o waar, ye micht say.

'Onywye, on the boat hame, queer things began happenin wi this desk. There wis voices in the middle o the nicht. Wailin voices. And then it took on this green kinna glow.'

'The supernatural powers,' said Mr Hartington-Partington.

'Well, the ither lads wis feart,' continued Sandy. 'They telt Dollop's faither he could keep the desk or they wid fling it ower the side.'

'And he kept it?' said Mr Hartington-Partington.

'He must hiv. For aul Dollop showed me it at the back o the chaumer at Mains.'

'He showed you it? Here?' Mr Hartington-Partington fumbled in his jacket pocket and brought out his wallet. His hands shook as he flicked through cards and receipts, and then produced a battered piece of card depicting a monstrous old piece of junk. He thrust the picture under Sandy's nose.

'Did it look like this?'

Sandy studied the picture. 'Oh, michty, michty,' he said. 'That's affa difficult tae say. I mean, it wis fifty year ago since I last saw it, and this isna an affa good drawin.'

'But do you think it looks like it?'

'Fae memory, it's real similar, bit . . .'

'Go on. Go on.'

'Well, there's nae muckle mair tae say. I went back that nicht and Dollop took me up til the chaumer and awa at the back, under an affa cobwebs, wis this aul dresser thing, covered in stue and hens' dirt and aathing.'

'D-did it have a central drawer?'

'I canna mind.'

'P-please concentrate. Do you think it had a central drawer, the one distinguishing feature of the chiagra?'

'I suppose it micht hiv haen.'

Mr Hartington-Partington clapped his hands together and turned to Mrs Barrington-Graham. 'A central drawer,' he squealed.

'Onywye,' said Sandy. 'We cleared aff the worst on the hens' dirt and blew aff as muckle o the stue as we could and we jist stood back and lookit at it. It wisna affa easy wi jist twa paraffin lumps; it bein dark and that. Ye ken fit happened next? The queerest thing.

'This bureau began glowin green. Then, affa faint at first, there wis a wailin got up. A tormentit kinna wailin. Lik the anguish o lost souls. Me bein a young loon, I wis real feart, bit aul Dollop jist stood there, defiant.'

Mr Hartington-Partington clutched Mrs Barrington-Graham's hand.

'Then the thing began tae shak. And there I wis, listenin til this anguished moanin and watchin this green glow and feelin this shak, shak, shakkin. And, Lord, three ghosts appeared oot o this bureau and they stared at Dollop and me, and we stared at them, and then they began wailin: 'Far are we? We're lost. Far are we? We're lost. Far are we? We're lost.'

'Really?' said Mr Hartington-Partington.

'Aye,' said Sandy. 'It wis a missin persons bureau.'

29 *Home from the Hospital*

IT was three days before Babbie Girn was allowed home from Inverspaver Cottage Hospital; her shoulder well wrapped up and with the sister's warning to be careful if she ventured out for her pension on icy pavements in future.

Babbie took the warning with good grace, but muttered to herself about institutional interference, then climbed into Walter Dreep's car for the eighteen-mile journey back to Stronach.

'Wis onything broken, Babbie?' inquired Walter as they bowled out of the hospital gates.

'Och, dinna ask,' said Babbie. 'The hale thing's been a pantomime fae stairt ti feenish. Pavements nae sattit. Ambulance late. Nae bed in the hospital. Roch brute o a doctor. Nae ambulance tae tak me hame. Fit's the country comin til?'

'Bit ye've nithing broken?'

'I may say that's mair luck than onything,' said Babbie. 'There's times I winder if the cooncils and the hospitals is mair concerned wi savin siller than makkin sure aathing's safe for aul bodies lik me.'

'Nivver mind, at least ye're gettin hame in plenty time for Christmas.'

'And foo will I manage Christmas wi this great muckle thing roon ma neck?' She shot a glare down at her strapped up arm and shoulder, to emphasise what an inconvenience it was.

Walter stopped the car in front of Babbie's home, which was now decorated with home-made bunting and emblazoned with the legend 'Welcome Home Babbie' in green paint on an old sheet strung from one of her upstairs windows.

'Look at that,' she said. 'Is it nae enough that I'm embarrassed aboot bein in hospital, athoot me bein black-affrontit haein an aul sheet hingin fae ma bedroom for the hale village's inspection? Ye're aa determined I'll be the spik o the place.'

Suitably chastened, Walter hopped out and round the back of the car in jig time to let Babbie out of the passenger door. She didn't have long to wait to see her next-door neighbour, for Virginia popped out of Babbie's own front door.

'Come awa, invalid,' said Virginia. 'I've a firie on and the kettle's biled. We'll hae a welcome-hame fly cup.'

'Ye can get that bliddy sheet doon afore ye dee onything else,' said Babbie, stamping past her neighbour and over the threshold. 'It's nae even clean.'

She disappeared inside, and Walter and Virginia looked at each other and shrugged. 'Thank ye onywye, Walter,' said Virginia, clapping his arm. 'It wis rale kind o ye takkin her hame. She's jist a bittie strung up the day.'

'She should be,' said Walter, turning to go.

Virginia closed the door and joined Babbie in the living-room.

'Foo are ye, quine?' she inquired.

'Och, dinna ask,' said Babbie. 'I'm sair. I've been rived at this past three days wi that roch brute o a consultant; I've been shoogled aa the road hame in that aul banger o Wattie's, and now I find I'm a lachin-stock wi an aul sheet hingin oot o ma bedroom.'

'We meant it for the best,' said Virginia. 'Fowk wis concerned aboot ye. If ye dinna mind me sayin, ye were a bittie roch on Wattie there. He did ye a gweed turn the day. We ken ye're wound up, bit ye mauna tak it oot on ither fowk.'

Babbie sat gingerly into the easy chair by the roaring fire. 'Ach, I ken,' she said. 'I'm ower aul for aa this capers. I jist wint a quaet life.'

'I dinna think ye'll hae muckle o a quaet life for the next day or twa,' said Virginia. 'There's flooers lik nithing on earth ben in the scullery. Aabody wis affa worried aboot ye. Ye'll likely hae veesitors.'

At that, the back door opened and in came Flo Spurtle. 'Coo-ee,' she cried. 'Only me. Foo's the invalid?'

'Och, dinna ask,' shouted Babbie as Flo made her way through. 'I'm jist nae masel ata. I've lost ma bloom.'

'Aye,' said Flo, studying her, 'richt enough. Yer bloom.'

They had time to say scarcely anything more when there was a knock at the front window, and there stood Geneva Brose. Virginia beckoned her round the back and presently Geneva, too, joined the assembly in the living-room.

'And are ye aaricht, Babbie?' she inquired, still breathless with the trot round the gable end.

'Och, dinna ask,' said Babbie. 'I widna wish it on onybody. It's jist been an affa experience aathegither.'

'Weel, if ye're needin ony help ata, jist lift the phone. Ye've nae need tae leave yer ain fireside til spring if need be.'

'It's a bruised shooder I've got,' said Babbie, 'nae twa broken legs. I'll be colleckin ma pinsion this wikk, as usual. It's lik faain aff a bike. If ye dinna get back on as quick's ye can, ye'll nivver go a bike again.'

Which was why Babbie came to be gripping Virginia's arm tightly as they stepped gingerly down to the Post Office two days later.

'Dinna worry, noo, quine,' soothed Virginia. 'There's nae ice. It's aa awa.'

'Ye're nivver sure,' said Babbie, concentrating hard on the pavement before her.

'Mrs Girn,' came a voice from across the road. It was the Rev. Montgomery Thole, and he crossed over to speak.

'And how are you today?'

'Och, dinna ask,' said Babbie. 'Dinna ask. It's takkin langer nor I thocht afore I'll be richt roadit.'

'Never you mind,' said Mr Thole brightly. 'You have good friends to look after you, I see. I'm sure you'll be as right as rain ere long. Good morning to you both.'

'Good morning,' said Babbie, as Mr Thole doffed his hat and went on his way. Then she stopped and, holding on to her chum, Virginia had to stop, too.

'Wid ye look at that?' said Babbie. Virginia peered down the street.

'It's the doctor,' said Virginia.

'Exackly,' said Babbie. 'Here's me been hame near three days and he's nivver lookit the road o me. Ma ain doctor. The man that's supposed ti tak an interest in the medical wellbein o the hale village, and here's me been in hospital and as far as he's concerned nithing's happened. Nivver visited. Nivver phoned. Nivver socht tae find oot aboot me. Nivver speired efter me. Nithing.'

'He's likely been busy, Babbie.'

'Foosht wi yer busy,' snapped Babbie. 'The least ye wid expect, if he couldna visit, wid be a phone call, speirin foo I am and if there's onything I needit. Did I get a phone call? Did I get a visit? Did I flech.

Look at that, he's climmin in ower his car and still nae lookin the road o me.'

But the doctor had, indeed, spotted Babbie, and he stepped out of his car at once and strode towards her.

'Mrs Girn,' he said, 'Mrs Girn. It's good to see you out and about so soon. Tell me, how are you feeling?'

'Och, doctor,' said Babbie. 'Dinna ask.'

30 *Bingo Night*

FLO Spurtle glanced to her right at Babbie Girn's bingo card. Seven numbers to go. Then she glanced to her left at Geneva Brose's. Five numbers. Then she looked down at her own.

With only one number left, she had been perspiring gently for fully a minute now. The back of her neck felt sticky and she longed to give it a rub to try to ease the tension, but she couldn't.

'Four and three, forty-three,' said the young caller. 'All the twos, twenty-two.'

'I'm jist waitin on one,' muttered Flo. 'Jist the one.'

Babbie looked across at Flo's card. 'Flo, ye're jist waitin on one.'

'On its own, number three,' cried the caller.

'I've been sittin like this for the past ten numbers,' said Flo. 'Ma insides is wound up tichter than an elastic band. I can hardly haud ma pen.'

'Five and eight, fifty-eight.'

Babbie leaned across Flo's front. 'Geneva. Ye hear that? Flo's jist waitin on ae number.'

Geneva peered at Flo's card and confirmed for herself that, indeed, only one of Flo's numbers was not crossed off.

'Six and three, sixty-three. Five-oh, blind fifty. On its own, number six.'

'Sivventeen,' urged Flo. 'One and sivven. Come on, sivventeen.'

'Three and nine, thirty-nine. Seven-oh, blind seventy. One and . . .' The caller broke into a fit of coughing and had to cover his mike as he boomed out over the public-address system.

Flo was leaning forward now. A buzz of disapproval from the clientele had drowned out what the caller had tried to say and it took a few moments for proceedings to return to normal. Then he announced:

'One and seven . . .'

'Houuuuuuuuuuussssse!' cried Flo, and she thrust her ticket into the air and flopped back into her seat. The perspiration had become a torrent of sweat. Geneva and Babbie were clapping her arms in congratulation, but Flo could hear only the thumping in her chest.

THEY spilled out of the bingo hall light of heart and of foot an hour and a half later. While the three of them admired the mock-leatherette briefcase-cum-portmanteau in which the winnings had been delivered (some promotion or other by the bingo company), Floretta, Geneva's daughter, drew up in the car, intending to act as taxi home.

The three older women had different ideas, however; they had decided already that they should go to celebrate their win with a port and lemon at one of Aberdeen's finest hostelries.

'And *we're* treatin *you*, Flo,' Geneva had insisted. 'We're nae haein ye burstin yer twa hunner and twenty poun. Nae wi it in sic a bonnie briefcase and aa.'

Thus, Floretta, Geneva, Babbie and Flo came to be whooping it up at a corner table at the Thumpin Heid Lounge and Function Suite; to such a degree that Flo's regular protestations that she had better be getting home soon fell on decidedly deaf ears. By 10.30, reasoning that Gibby would be already in bed, even Flo gave up and settled into the wild spirit of a girls' night out.

When eventually they did decide to brave the Aberdeen cold once more, and teetered up the street, giggling fit to match any teenager, it was only a shade before midnight.

Floretta, having stuck to lemonades all evening, had the unenviable task of trying to shoehorn two ample matrons and a middle-aged woman into a Mini. So comic was it, that Geneva had to ask to be excused to go back to visit the facilities.

By the time they reboarded and set off, and were coursing through the suburbs heading for Stronach, it was already closer to 1am than to midnight.

The giggly effects of all those ports and lemon had emboldened Flo, perhaps a little more than was wise.

'I'll fling open the bedroom door,' she slurred. 'I'll fling open the bedroom door and I'll teem that little briefcase ower his heid and aa that siller'll flutter ower him and I'll say: 'There ye go, big boy. Fit dis it feel like tae be mairriet til a filthy-rich wife?'

'And fit'll he say?' asked Geneva.

'He'll say: "Pit oot that licht and stop caperin aboot. I've tae be up early the morn."'

The four of them hooted with laughter as the Mini headed into the hills.

THEY didn't drop Flo off outside her house. Flo thought that the noise of the car engine would waken Gibby and children, to say nothing of the neighbours, so she was dropped in the village centre, whispered her goodbyes, took her leatherette briefcase and began striding for home.

She pushed open the garden gate slowly to minimise the squeak and, working from memory in the dark, tiptoed round the front of the house, up the side and turned towards the back door.

She negotiated the steps perfectly well but, fumbling for her key, managed somehow to drop the briefcase. It clattered down what seemed like each one of the four steps in that noisy way which makes the tiniest sounds seem like explosions late at night.

Flo steeled herself for lights to be switched on, if not in their own house, then certainly in some of the neighbours'. But there was nothing.

She gripped the back-door handle for a moment or two to steady herself – those ports and lemon had been a little more potent and longer-lasting than she would have liked – then she fumbled once more in all her pockets, trying to find her key.

For an anxious moment, she wondered if it might have slipped from her pocket in the Mini, but then, as is often the way in mounting panic, the key turned up, tucked in a seam at the bottom of her inside pocket.

She managed to get it in the lock at the third attempt and opened the door gently. She fumbled for the lightswitch and flicked it on. She hauled herself inside, shut the door and climbed upstairs to bed.

GIBBY said nothing about his wife's late homecoming. The first Flo knew that morning had arrived was in becoming conscious of the empty space beside her and the whistling and clattering in the kitchen downstairs. She peered at the alarm. Six-thirty.

She was lying there, trying to come to herself and not wanting to move too quickly in case the port and lemon kicked in again, when she remembered vaguely that the briefcase and her win had tumbled down the back steps as she had arrived, but she couldn't recall actually bringing her booty inside.

She tried vainly to remember where in the house she might have put it but, despite several slow-motion replays, had to come to the conclusion that she had left the prize outside overnight.

That was when she heard a wail from somewhere down below, followed quickly by the thump and bang of Gibby thundering up the stairs two at a time.

The bedroom door burst open. 'Flo! Flo!,' he said.

He was beaming and excited. 'Ye'll nivver guess fit there is at the back door.'

She propped herself up on her elbow and squinted against the light at her husband.

'I ken,' she said wearily. 'Afore ye start, I ken. I should hiv telt ye last nicht fin I got hame, bit it wis a bittie late and ye were sleepin. Ye've found twa hunner and twinty poun in notes and a bonnie leatherette briefcase.'

Gibby stepped forward. 'No,' he said. 'Fower hunner and twinty-three bottles o milk.'

31 *Erchie Goes Fishing*

IT had been a slow morning, but Erchie was none too bothered about that. He had savoured the crispness of a March dawn, the walk up to the top end of the Water of Stronach, and the knowledge that he was enjoying the solitude of the vale while, below him, the village was still sleeping.

He had caught nothing much, but the process of fishing was more important than the result to Erchie. It gave him time to think things through and to lay plans.

This morning, he was wrestling with the problem of Sammy Dreep's future. The lad appeared to have lost his confidence, thought Erchie. Decisiveness was the quality he lacked, and Erchie needed to find a way to boost Sammy's self-esteem.

So absorbed had he been in Sammy's future that he had quite forgotten to take with him his usual fishing-trip comestibles. While he had all the angling paraphernalia, he had nothing much to sustain him in the food department. More worrying than that, he had left behind his half-bottle on the kitchen table.

He fumbled in his dungars for a minute or so and discovered a half-eaten fig roll deep in one pooch. He had no idea of its vintage, but it looked reasonably fresh and, once he had brushed off the worst of the fluff and garden grit, moderately edible, so he ate it.

Fifteen minutes later, he was as peckish as before and toyed with the idea of abandoning his outing and returning home. Besides, weren't the clouds gathering behind the Hill of Stronach, and weren't they scudding his way?

Erchie turned up his collar and tried to concentrate on the water. He was interrupted minutes later by the sound of a car engine labouring down the dirt road. Presently, Godfrey Barrington-Graham's Volvo estate-car hove in sight.

It crested the small rise onto the plateau of the burnside, wheeled round and parked in an alcove of whinns. Mr Barrington-Graham evidently had not noticed Erchie, for he was singing: 'I am the sunshine of my life' as he climbed out and strode round to the tailgate.

He hauled out rods, nets and the first of three wicker baskets, all the while studied by his fellow-villager.

It was only when he turned round to pick himself a spot that he noticed Erchie beaming back at him. Mr Barrington-Graham's smile froze.

'It's yersel,' said Erchie.

'Indeed,' said Mr Barrington-Graham.

'It'll be fine tae hae company.'

'Um, well, I wouldn't want to cramp your style. Shall I just go a little further up the bank?'

'Suit yersel,' said Erchie. 'Though ye winna likely catch nithing up by there. The best o them's usually doon hereaboots.'

'Nevertheless, nothing ventured, nothing gained, eh?' Mr Barrington-Graham began the first of several ferry trips from the back of his car to a spot fifty yards or so upstream.

'I nivver thocht ee'd be oot fishin on a Tuesday mornin,' said Erchie. 'Are ye nae workin the day?'

'I've taken the rest of the week off,' said Mr Barrington-Graham, lumbering towards the burnside with the biggest wicker basket on his hip. 'We landed rather an important contract at the weekend and, frankly, I think I deserve a little time to myself after so much burning the midnight oil. The fresh air and a little solitude I thought would be the perfect antidote.'

'I like solitude masel,' said Erchie.

It took Mr Barrington-Graham another fifteen minutes to set himself up to his satisfaction; a procedure which entertained Erchie greatly. By the time Mr Barrington-Graham had first cast and had settled back in his leather-faced stool, all the fish would have been scared off by the racket, thought Erchie.

They sat there in silence, fifty yards apart, for more than half an hour. The clouds that had threatened rain were still there, still threatening, but coming to nothing much. A wind from the north-west had whipped up and made Erchie raise his anorak collar a little higher. Mr Barrington-Graham merely pulled up the zip another couple of inches on his fleece-lined Berghaus weatherproof.

They had just heard eight faint chimes floating up from the village kirk when Mr Barrington-Graham reached into one of his wicker baskets and hauled out a linen-wrapped parcel. From inside came a couple of rounds of sandwiches; fish, by the smell, thought Erchie.

'Aye,' he said. 'It's fairly hungry wark, the fishin.'

'Certainly is,' said Mr Barrington-Graham through a mouthful of granary bread. He reached for another.

'I aye find a sandwich helps keep oot the caul.'

'Couldn't agree more. This smoked salmon's delicious, may I say. Katharine has it dispatched specially from our favourite delicatessen in Islington. It's a little more expensive, but the flavour is so delicate that we feel it's worth it.'

'I wid bet,' said Erchie. 'I like a tinnie o John West. If ye pit an egg throwe't, ye can stretch it tae twa denners. I've aye windered fit smoked salmon tastes lik in a sandwich.'

'Delicious, I do assure you,' said Mr Barrington-Graham. He reached for the last sandwich and took a bite.

'That's a comfort, than,' said Erchie.

They continued for another fifteen minutes, the temperature dropping noticeably, when Mr Barrington-Graham reached into his wicker basket again. He produced a short tumbler, then what appeared to be a silver hipflask. Erchie did not mistake the light scent of a Macallan thirty-year-old.

Mr Barrington-Graham sniffed the handsome measure he had poured, smiled to himself, then took a swig.

'Aah,' he said, smacking his lips and breathing hard, 'that helps to keep out the cold.'

'Caul up far you are, is't?' said Erchie. 'I'm sure it couldna be muckle warmer doon here.'

'It is quite chilly, yes,' said Mr Barrington-Graham, screwing the cap back on the flask and slipping into his weatherproof's poacher's pocket.

'I'm sympathetic for ye,' said Erchie, turning back to gaze at the water.

Twenty minutes later, Mr Barrington-Graham reached back into the poacher's pocket for another dram.

'Caul again?' said Erchie.

'Freezing,' said Mr Barrington-Graham. He took another swig. 'I sometimes wonder why I bother fishing.'

111

'Me tee,' said Erchie. He looked towards the Hill of Stronach, where the clouds were noticeably darker. 'Looks lik rain.'

'To misquote the song,' said Mr Barrington-Graham, 'I've got my malt to keep me warm.'

The rain arrived half an hour later; a light drizzle at first, but soon building from spirks and spots into a steady shower.

Mr Barrington-Graham popped up a huge angler's umbrella. Erchie, meanwhile, already had turned up his collar as far as it would go and was left with no more protection.

He began to pack up for the long and wet walk back to the village when he noticed Mr Barrington-Graham fumbling in the wicker basket again.

It was a pipe this time. Mr Barrington-Graham tapped it full of some Dutch tobacco, then pulled out a box of matches. Alas, despite numerous attempts, the matches would not work. He tried the matchbox, the back of his heel and the top of a nearby stone, to no avail.

'Trouble crackin yer spunks, Mr Barrington-Graham?' observed Erchie.

'I beg your pardon?'

'Yer matches. Ye canna get a licht?'

'Apparently not,' said Mr Barrington-Graham, 'and it's so frustrating. I like my pipe at this time in the morning. You don't know anywhere dry I could strike a match, do you?'

'Weel,' said Erchie, packing his fishing-rod into the crook of his arm, 'ye could hiv tried the back o ma throat.'

32 *Gibby's New Nephew*

FLO Spurtle looked at her watch and then at the clock above the sideboard. They agreed perfectly on the time, just as they had when last she had checked four minutes previously. She walked through to the kitchen and stood at the window, listening to the sounds of hammering and sawing from the shed by the back door.

For a moment, she thought about making herself another cup of tea while she waited, but then she looked at her watch again and headed outside. She had to wait for a second or two before Gibby, swathed in sawdust and wielding an electric drill now, spotted her. He simply nodded an acknowledgement and went back to his carpentry.

Flo marched inside and unplugged the drill. The shed fell silent. Gibby looked up, saw how displeased she was and slipped off his earmuffs.

'Ye've unplugged me,' he said.

Flo tapped her watch. 'Ye promised we'd be awa at half past two,' she said. 'It's now a quaarter til. Ye hinna time tae get yersel tidied up and riggit afore we've tae be awa.'

'It's only a new bairn we're gaun tae see,' said Gibby. He began tracing the cord of drill, intending to plug it back in. 'Ye see ae new bairn, ye've seen them aa.'

'It's my sister's new bairn,' said Flo. 'Yer nephew. The latest addition tae wir faimly and you canna steer yersel tae be interestit. Ye'd raither stick here in this dingy hole o a shed and knock up mair rubbish.'

'It's nae rubbish,' said Gibby. He looked hurt. 'This is the latest design o magazine rack. Hauds a hale year's worth o *Gardeners' World*, or a wikk's *Press and Journals*. If this works, it'll be anither string tae ma ivver-expandin bow.'

'If this works it'll be a miracle,' said Flo. She stepped forward. 'Ye've been workin on this magazine rack for a wikk and a half now.

Ye've put in maybe twinty, thirty oors. Gibby, ye can *buy* a magazine rack in Woolies for a tenner.'

'Nae the same workmanship, though,' he said.

'I agree,' said Flo. 'It's better. I'm sorry tae be brutal aboot it, bit jinerin's nivver been a talent o yours. For thirty oors' work, ye'll finish up wi a tenner's worth o result.'

'Bit it's the pleasure o creatin something wi yer ain hands,' said Gibby. 'Ye canna pit a price on that.'

THE visit was every bit as awkward as Gibby knew it would be. He sat, uncomfortable in his Sunday best, fidgeting on the edge of the sofa while Flo and her sister compared notes about the first few weeks of motherhood.

'And ye're sure the baby's OK oot in that sun?' Flo was asking.

'Mercy, of coorse,' said her sister. 'The canopy's up and it's a fine widden rocker-crib. They dinna keep the heat the same.'

Gibby stood up. 'Ye dinna mind if I ging oot and tak a look at yer gairden, div ye?' he said and stepped awkwardly past the two women and disappeared outside.

'He's nae affa settled, is he?' said Flo's sister once Gibby had gone. 'He's nivver been affa outgoin, bit I've nivver kent him as dry as this.'

'Tae be honest,' said Flo, 'and dinna tak this the wrang wye, bit he wisna really wintin tae come here the day. It's nithing personal. Gibby's nivver hid an affa interest in babies and bairns. This is his idea o purgatory, I suppose: a hale aifterneen o natterin aboot nappies.'

'Bit ye've twa kids o yer ain,' said Flo's sister. 'Surely he took an interest in them.'

'An interest,' said Flo. 'Bit ye widna describe him as hands-on. Some men's geared up for bein faithers and ithers jist canna get tae grips.'

'Nae even that first time he saw his ain wee loonie lookin up at him?'

Flo had to think for a second. 'No, I dinna think he wis emotional ata. Nae even a moistness aboot the een. It wis nearly as if it wisna his bairn.'

'That's affa that,' said Flo's sister.

'Oh, he loves his bairns,' said Flo. 'He widna see nithing comin ower them, bit he disna get saft aboot them. Typical Scot.'

'Did ye nivver try geein him up?'

'I tried aathing for the first twa–three month,' said Flo. 'I wid find ony excuse tae pit the bairn in his airms, tae see if that wid spark something. It nivver did. I suppose Gibby's jist got ither interests. Onywye, we've been stickin aboot in here and missin aa this sunshine. Will we go oot and hae a tekkie roon the gairden and see if we've ony straaberries?'

They were almost out at the back door when Flo's sister halted and put out an arm to stop Flo. She nodded over to the left side of the garden and the little patch of grass beyond the vegetable patch.

There, Flo saw, stood Gibby, peering down into the rocker crib, wide-eyed and enchanted.

Flo's sister looked round. 'I thocht ye said he'd nae interest in bairns.'

Gibby was just standing there, gazing down and smiling. He was saying nothing; his arms stuffed firmly in his pockets, but the look on his face was unmistakable. He stooped to peer inside the crib, and put his hand on the edge. He had his back to them now, so they could not see.

Flo and her sister, stepped quietly from the house and down the path, watching Gibby all the time.

They were almost upon him before he realised he was being watched and he stood up sharply, as if caught red-handed.

'So ye like yer nephew, Gibby?' said Flo's sister.

'We saw ye,' said Flo. She grasped his elbow. 'We saw ye booin doon and lachin til him.'

'I did nae sic thing,' Gibby said.

'Dinna tell lees,' said Flo's sister. 'It's real nice tae see somebody takkin a shine til a new baby. Especially a man that disna hae muckle time for babies. We saw the excitement and the amazement and the enchantment on yer face.'

'A penny for yer thochts,' said Flo.

Gibby turned and reached into the inside lip of the crib. He drew out a label on a piece of string. 'I wis jist stannin here winderin how they can mak a rare widden crib like this for £32.99.'

33 *How to Get Rich*

FLO Spurtle tossed the little scrap of card in the litter bin, then turned back to Ebenezer Grip. 'I assume fae yer face that ye winna be awa on a cruise til the Bahamas next wikk,' he said.

'Gie the man a coconut,' said Flo. 'No, yet again, ma luck's richt oot. I've deen the Lottery ilky wikk since it startit, and I've bocht scratchcards fanivver I could affoord them, and fit hiv I won? A tenner last December. That's aa.'

'Nivver mind, Flo,' said Ebenezer. 'Look at the bricht side. Here you are on yer knees daily-day cleanin ither fowk's hooses and home-helpin and scrapin and savin for yer twa Lottery ticketies a wikk, and yer siller's gaun til really needy causes lik the Royal Opera Hoose in London, so aa the nobs wi their fur coats and Rolls-Royces can hae chaep tickets ti hear big fat wifies scraichin and wailing aboot nithing ava.'

'I like tae dee ma bit,' said Flo.

LOTTERY fever died a little at Stronach just two days later when Kate Barrington-Graham stuck a poster on the community-council notice-board outside the village hall. It took an hour or two for word to get round, for no one reads community-council noticeboards, but soon little knots of two or three people were gathering to read.

Money. Money. Money.
How to Get Rich
Come and hear how it's done from someone who knows.
Meet top entrepreneur Harry Andersen, a multimillionaire
with three yachts, homes in 10 of the world's major cities,
a fleet of Bentleys and his own private jet.
Andersen will offer tips at a seminar in the hall next
Tuesday evening at 7.30pm.
All welcome. Bring own teaspoon.

Over the next five days, Stronach buzzed with excitement that a multimillionaire would be visiting the village and that easy riches awaited those who followed his free advice.

By the time Tuesday evening came, seats in the village hall were at a premium and a long queue snaked down the street to the village fountain, necks all craning to see what chance they might have of gaining entry to hear the great man.

Eventually, Erchie Sotter, the hallkeeper, grabbed the Emergency Exit bar and began pulling the doors shut, to groans of protest from those who had not made the cut.

Within minutes, a champagne-gold Rolls-Royce bowled up at the front and the crowd turned en masse to catch a glimpse of the passengers. First, out stepped Mr and Mrs Barrington-Graham, then came their weekend guest, a short, stocky man with an immaculate haircut, Pyper Marlborough suit and an astrakhan coat slung across his shoulders.

While the Barrington-Grahams basked in reflected glory as they made their way through the crowd, Mr Andersen followed in their wake, smiling at the villagers who had gathered, but who were disappointed that their quarry did not appear to be particularly famous.

Once Godfrey-Barrington Graham had introduced Mr Andersen with a welcome speech so embarrassing and crawling that it was clear that he was after a contract, Mr Andersen slipped off his coat, unbuttoned his suit and strode to the makeshift podium.

'Good evening,' he said. His accent was foreign. Although polished by years of speaking English, it was clear that Mr Andersen was not British-born.

'I hope you'll excuse me,' he continued, 'but I am not accustomed to speaking in public. In fact, I don't think I have ever spoken to the general public before. Most of my speeches are business proposals and such things. I hope this evening won't waste your time.

'Some of you will have detected a slight accent. Therein lies the root of my success. I was a Hungarian refugee in 1956. I fled to this country with nothing but the suit on my back, the shoes on my feet and two paper bags.

'Within four years, I had fourteen companies, two homes in London and one in New York, an annual group turnover of five million pounds and had a collection of paintings and Chinese ceramics insured for at least ten million.

'How I did it is no great mystery. How did a poor little Hungarian boy with two paper bags come to find such fortune? That's what I propose to relate.'

For the next twenty minutes, the audience sat enraptured as Mr Andersen told a potted life story of hard work and acumen and exploiting opportunity. Then he invited questions. At the back of the hall, Erchie Sotter called:

'Excuse me, Mr Andersen,' he said. 'This is maybe nae the kinna question ye're sikkin, bit did ye keep yer paper bags?'

'Why, as a matter of fact, I did,' said Mr Anderson. 'I had them framed and they hang in my penthouse suite in my New York building. They remind me that I came with nothing and that, at any minute, like any entrepreneur, I might find myself with nothing once more. Wealth is transient sir; a fickle mistress.'

'It's jist that, fin I wis in the waar,' said Erchie. 'I'd twa paper bags masel, bit there wis nivver nithing come o't.'

'Well, sometimes it falls to Lady Luck, sir. Who has another question?'

But Erchie was not for shaking. 'The thing is,' he continued, 'it's funny you mentionin paper bugs, because there's an affa lotta boys efter the waar made good oot o nithing ata.'

'I believe so. It was a time when enterprise was its own reward.'

'I come across een nae lang efter we invadit Italy. He wis an Italian boy in their Resistance, and he wis fleein the fascists and he'd nithing bit twa paper bugs and he socht passage back ti Blighty efter the war. We telt him we'd fairly help him if he wid help us. So he telt us aa the inside griff on fit Mussolini's boys wis up til, and we roundit them up in nae time ata.

'And seein as the boy wis as good as his word, we took him in and lookit efter him and, eventually, he got back til Blighty wi's. And he hid nithing bit the claes on his back and the sheen on his feet and his twa paper bugs.'

'And was he successful in his new life, sir?'

'I wyte he wis successful,' said Erchie. 'He'd a coupla rolled-up Rembrandts in ae bag and three hunder thoosan poun in used notes in the ither.'

34 Remember the Pigeon Corps

ERCHIE Sotter reached for the door-knocker, rapped sharply three times and stood back. 'Fit Fobbie Pluffer disna ken aboot doos is nae worth kennin,' he assured Walter Dreep. 'I whiles think he wis amon doos in his pram, he's that weel acquant wi them.'

'I hinna said for certain that I'm takkin up doo-keepin as a hobby,' said Walter, alarmed that events had accelerated beyond his control. 'For a start, Aggie'll likely hae something tae say, and I've a fair idea I ken fit the something'll be.'

'Pit yer fit doon,' said Erchie. 'She's yer wife, nae yer maister.'

He stepped forward and rapped at the door again. 'He's maybe takkin a forty winks,' he said. 'Us aul boys gets affa easy tired.'

Walter turned to go. 'We winna wakken him, than,' he said, but Erchie grabbed his elbow and propelled him along the front of the house towards the gable end.

'If Fobbie's nae snoozin, he'll be in his doocot,' he said. 'I telt ye he wis dedicatit.'

As Erchie had said, Forbes Pluffer was, indeed, in his doocot, chatting to his beloved pigeons as if they were children; cradling and stroking them; holding them up to the skylight to admire their form from every angle.

'Fobbie,' said Erchie, striding across the drying-green and hauling Walter in his wake. 'Fobbie, I micht hiv kent I wid find ye wi yer doos. This man here's sikkin some advice, isn't that richt, Wattie?'

'Jist advice,' stressed Walter.

'Aboot doos,' said Erchie. 'Wattie's thinkin o takkin up doo-keepin as a hobby.'

'A gran hobby, richt enough,' said Fobbie, 'bit most affa time-consumin if ye dee't richt. Tae my mind, if ye're nae intendin deein't richt, ye needna bother.'

'I wid fairly dee't richt,' said Walter, mildly insulted. 'I dinna start nithing at half-cock. If I wisna intendin deein it richt, I widna hiv come here tae fin oot richt aboot them, wid I?'

'Ask awa than,' said Fobbie, carefully slipping a pigeon into its enclosure.

'Fit div ye get oot o't?' said Walter. 'I mean, ye canna tak them for walks, and they canna hae muckle personality.'

'Nae personality?' said Fobbie. 'Nae personality? Wattie, I've forty-five doos in here and they've aa different personalities. There's ill-trickit doos. There's lazy doos. There's hungry doos. There's fleet doos, bonnie doos, clivver doos, gawpit doos. There's as muckle personality in doos as there is in humans.' He turned to survey the assorted heads blinking and cooin back at him. 'In fact,' he said, 'there's aften I think they've maybe mair personality than ony o's.'

'Div they nae mak an affa mess?' said Walter. 'I couldna thole a mess. Especially on washin-day.'

'Aggie widna like it, eh?' said Fobbie.

'No, I dee the washin,' said Walter. '*I* widna like it. Nithing waur nor doos doin dos aa ower yer doins. Gad sakes.'

'They're as clean as ye let them be,' said Fobbie. 'If ye spen time wi them and treat them wi respect and look efter them, they're the cleanest animals ye'll ivver come across. Aa this stories ye hear aboot skitter ower the heid, that's jist a sign that the mannie that keeps them is nae deein his job. He's nae takkin a pride in his doos. He's nae got a sense o responsibility.'

'Foo muckle time div ye spen' ilky day wi yer doos?' said Walter.

'I'm oot as seen as it's licht, mair or less. There's aye something needs deein for them. It's a shortsome day, deein for doos, richt enough.'

'And dis it cost a lot?'

'Jist the feed. I've nivver nott a vet for ony emergency in aa ma time keepin doos. It aa depends on foo mony doos ye keep, of coorse. Ye dinna hae tae start aff wi mair than forty lik me. Start aff wi half a dizzen and see if ye like the idea.'

'I'll need tae see if Aggie likes the idea afore I dee onything,' said Walter.

Fobbie unlatched a cage and lifted out one of the pigeons, which he offered to Walter. 'Try her for size,' he said. 'This is Marigold. She's a Normandy Blue and she's got a richt bonnie nater.'

Walter took the pigeon from Fobbie and marvelled at how silky and warm it was.

'Of coorse,' said Fobbie. 'I dinna ken fit wye ye're comin here and askin *me* aboot doos. Fit wye did ye nae ask the expert?'

'Fitna expert?' said Walter, looking up.

'Yer mate here. Erchie.'

Walter looked round. 'I didna ken you kent aboot doos, Erchie,' he said.

Erchie stammered. 'Me? Doos?'

'Come on, Erchie,' said Fobbie. 'Dinna be bashful. Tell Wattie aboot yer exploits wi the Pigeon Corps in France durin the war. Jist like ye telt me thon nicht in the pub.'

'The Pigeon Corps?' said Walter, looking at Erchie.

'Eh, oh, aye. The Pigeon Corps,' said Erchie. 'We wis a gey hush-hush kinna outfit.'

'Fit did ye dee in this Pigeon Corps?' said Walter.

'Tell him, Erchie,' said Fobbie. 'Tell him foo ye trained doos for drappin grenades on enemy positions.'

'Doos cairryin grenades?' said Walter.

'Did I nae tell ye doos wis brainy?' said Fobbie, positively glowing with pride.

'Foo did they manage pullin oot the preen?' said Walter.

'Eh, special grenades,' said Erchie. 'On a lang delay.'

'Surely affa risky,' said Walter, smiling.

'Only the once, isn't that richt, Erchie?' said Fobbie. 'The time ye said a doo got lost and cam back hame still wi the live grenade. You saved sivven o yer mates by flingin yer tin hat ower the trap o't.'

'Eh, aye. That's richt. Aye.' said Erchie. 'We aa shiftit wirsels quick that mornin.'

'Far aboot did aa this happen?' said Walter. 'France, ye said?'

'Eh, aye, a little villagie half-wye atween Rouen and Epernay.'

'Now, now, now, Erchie,' said Fobbie. 'Ye're most affa bashful the day. Tell the story richt. Tell him foo yer wartime exploits wi The Pigeon Corps in France helped develop the Doric.'

'Helped develop the Doric?' said Walter.

'It wis in a little village atween Rouen and Epernay that the secret headquarters o the Pigeon Corps wis locatit,' said Fobbie. 'The little village o Fouzière, half-wye up a hillside. A bonnie little place, Erchie said. Wisn't it a bonnie little place, Erchie?'

'Eh, aye.'

'And – go on, tell Wattie – ye chose Fouzière because it wis that sma and that bonnie that the Nazis wid nivver hiv thocht o lookin there for a top-secret set-oot, isn't that richt?'

'That's richt, aye,' said Erchie. 'Well, Wattie, it's aboot time we wis awa.'

'Jist a mintie, Erchie,' said Walter. 'Far dis the Doric connection come in?'

'Come, come, Wattie,' said Fobbie. 'And ye ca yersel a Stronach man? Can ye believe this, Erchie? Can ye believe the ignorance o some fowk?

'Walter, ye've surely heard o the Fouzière Doos.'

35 *Babbie on her Bike*

ERCHIE Sotter set the can of oil down beside him then leaned back to survey his work. 'Weel, Babbie,' he said, 'I've deen the best I can, bit I canna see yer bike gaun muckle farrer than the end o the road. It's hardly this year's model.'

Standing at a safe distance behind Erchie, Babbie Girn looked at her old sit-up-and-beg pushbike and sighed. 'Maybe no,' she said, 'bit I maun get fitter ae wye or anither afore I set aff on this cruise. I'm nae spennin aa that siller and lyin on ma bed in ma cabin day in, day oot. The doctor telt me exercise wis the thing and I'm takkin his advice. That bittie in the paper said bikin wis rare exercise and here's me wi a bike in ma ain shed nae deein nithing.'

'I'm nae sure the paper meant that fowk near sivventy should tak the heid o the road on a pushbike fae the last waar, though, Babbie,' said Erchie, hauling himself up.

'Are ye sayin it winna go?'

'It'll rin fine,' said Erchie. 'I've iled it. I've kittled up yer chine. I've replaced yer brakes. The seat's a bittie past its best bit, then, sae's yer ain.'

Babbie ignored the barb. 'And foo muckle div I owe ye?'

'Not a bean, Babbie,' he said. 'Nae a brass maik. Jist sen' ben a bowlie o yer fine broth the next time ye've a makkin.'

He walked towards the small gate in their mutual fence, then stopped. 'Jist ae thing,' he said. 'Be sure and mak yer broth afore ye g'awa on yer bike. That thing could be the feenish o ye.'

Later that afternoon, Virginia Huffie appeared for her customary fly cup and Babbie ushered her out to the shed to view the rejuvenated bicycle. Virginia was as sceptical as Erchie had been.

'Can ye go a bike at your age, Babbie? Especially a bike lik that.'

'Ye ken fit they say,' said Babbie. 'Naebody nivver forgets foo tae go a bike. It's lik watter aff a deuk. Mark my words, Virginia; I'll seen be crunkin her up the tap road and doon the low road lik a hen ower a midden. Ye winna see me for stue and sma steens.'

'I admire ye, Babbie,' said Virginia, eyeing the bicycle warily as if she were staring at Babbie's nemesis. 'Takkin up bikin in yer aul age taks real smeddum. Or something. Ye're nae headin oot the day, are ye?'

'Eh, no,' said Babbie, trying to steer Virginia back to the house. 'I thocht I'd wait a filie for the fine days.'

Virginia looked at the vivid-blue sky, the sharp shadows across the garden and wiped a light sheen of perspiration from her brow. 'Richt enough, Babbie,' she said. 'Ye widna wint tae risk a chill.'

VIRGINIA steered clear of the subject of bicycles and fitness for the next few days and Babbie did not raise the matter again. The whole subject of their cruise did not arise until the following Monday, when Babbie wondered if she might go on a diet.

'I dinna think so, Babbie,' said Virginia as gently as she could. 'It's nae as if ye'll be gaun aboot in a bikini, is it? It disna really maitter for a puckle lirky bits at oor age. A cardigan covers a multitude o sins.'

'Ye dinna wint tae g'awa on yer hol'days feelin the same as ye feel at hame, though,' said Babbie. 'I could maybe loase a coupla pun here and there, div ye think?'

'If ye really think so,' said Virginia.

Babbie snorted. 'Ye dinna like ma bike idea. Ye dinna like ma diet idea. I dinna think ye like the thocht o me enjoyin ma holiday.'

'It's nae that,' said Virginia. 'Not at all. Bit ye winna enjoy yer holiday if ye're tired oot wi bikin and dietin. Could ye nae prepare for the cruise deein something a bittie less strenuous?'

'Like fit?'

Virginia thought for a moment, then brightened. 'Fit aboot a new frock?'

'A new frock? Fit need hiv I o a new frock? I'd a new frock fae Isaac Benzie nae lang ago.'

'Isaac Benzie shut aboot twinty year ago, Babbie.'

'And it's a frock that's nivver been on,' said Babbie.

'Well, if it's nae a new frock, fit aboot a perm?'

Babbie thought for a moment, then stood up and walked across to the mirror above the sideboard. She removed her hairnet and turned her head this way and that, trying to judge the lie of her locks, until she turned round to Virginia.

'Weel,' she said. 'It's maybe some early yet for thinkin aboot a perm bit, the wye I see it, if onything gings wrang wi the first een, there's aye time for a repair job afore we set aff for the Mediterranean.'

Virginia smiled. 'That's the spirit,' she said.

BABBIE took nobody with her to the Frizz and Fronds Unisex Salon and Manicure Parlour on Inverspaver High Street. Not even Virginia. She wanted the experiment to be conducted in absolute secrecy, lest anything go awry.

When she settled back in the chair, pop music blaring at her from the radio-cassette on the shelf in front of her, she swallowed hard and instructed the young stylist to do what she thought fit. Then hardly daring to look in the mirror as large chunks of lank curls were pulled straight and painted with a foul-smelling paste.

The two hours crept by painfully slowly until, eventually, Babbie felt able to look up into the mirror.

The face staring back at her was hardy recognisable. She studied the change for a few seconds than could scarcely stop herself breaking out into broad grin.

'Ye like it?' said the stylist, knowing perfectly well from Babbie's grin that she liked it.

'It dis something for me, aye,' said Babbie, looking this way and that. 'It's nae bad ata, lassie. Ye've deen real weel.'

Babbie shochled out of her seat, slipped into her coat and paid her bill. She gave the stylist a 20p tip and the stylist wished her a safe and pleasant holiday. Babbie left the salon and headed for the bus stop feeling at least fifteen years younger. She almost broke into a wee tune.

The bus arrived on time and left on time, and Babbie found herself urging the driver to speed up so that she could be back in plenty of time for the shops to be open so that she could just happen to go buying a few little essentials that she had happened to forget, preferably with two or three other customers around at the same time.

She almost danced down the steps of the bus as it halted outside the Emporium. She waited for the bus to pull away, then crossed the road as quickly as she could, bearing down on the Emporium front door. She had just grasped the handle when she heard a shout from behind her. It was Erchie Sotter.

'Oh, hello, Erchie,' she said, standing up so that he had a good view of the new coiffure.

'Babbie,' he said. 'Is there something different aboot ye?'

She smiled. 'Div ye think so?' she said.

'There's fairly something aboot yer hair,' said Erchie. He studied her for a few seconds more, then snapped his fingers.

'I've got it,' he said. 'Hiv ye been oot on yer bike?'

36 Erchie's Musical Heritage

ANYONE who spotted Erchie Sotter rushing through the evening snowfall might have been a little surprised by his haste. Coat done up against the wind, he was stooping and tripping among puddles more quickly than any Stronach resident might have expected of a man of seventy-six; especially of Erchie.

Had they looked a little more closely as he had stepped off the last bus from Inverspaver, they might have noticed, in the dull orange glow of the streetlights, that the front of his coat seemed bulked out more than usual.

This was because Erchie was returning home with a bargain.

He passed the welcoming lights of the Stronach Arms with nary a second thought. Had he known how concerned they had been about his non-arrival that night, he might have considered stopping by to say hello, but Erchie had other thoughts on his mind.

He reached the terrace a couple of minutes later and headed not for his own front door, but for that of his neighbour, Babbie Girn.

Babbie seemed decidedly irritated to see him.

'What a trouble ye've caused the nicht, Sotter,' she told him, but she stepped aside to let him in. 'I thocht ye usually telt fowk at the pub if ye'd ither plans ony nicht. Fin ye didna turn up the nicht, they sent up twa fowk tae see that ye were aaricht. They were worried aboot ye. I couldna help them, because I didna ken far ye were, eether.'

Erchie motioned her to shut the living-room door.

'I wis at Inverspaver,' he said. 'I'm jist new back aff the last bus.'

'Fit wye are ye whisperin?'

Erchie cleared his throat. 'I'm needin advice,' he said.

'I see,' Babbie said. 'Fit's that aneth yer coat?'

'That's fit I'm needin the advice aboot.' Erchie undid the coat carefully and produced a thick brown-paper parcel. Babbie studied it, then studied him. 'If we're playin pass the parcel, we need mair fowk,' she said.

Erchie untied the string and peeled back the paper with a delicacy which suggested something of great value inside. Moments later, he pulled back the last sheet to reveal:

'A fiddle?' Babbie said.

'Nae a fiddle,' Erchie said. 'A violin. And nae jist ony violin. A Stradivarius.'

'I didna ken ye played the fiddle.'

'I dinna, bit I couldna ignore a bargain like this.'

'I ken nithing aboot fiddles,' Babbie said.

'Bit ye ken aboot windfall antiques,' Erchie said. 'Sivven year ago, your aul tattie-pot turned oot tae be a valuable bit o porcelain and ye made hunners o thoosans aff o't.'

'Nivver you mind aboot my aul tattie-pot.'

'The question is, far div I get this valued?'

'Ony antique shop wid be a good start,' Babbie said. 'Are ye expeckin it tae be worth a lotta money, like?'

'The boy said at least three hunner thoosan. He said it maybe wisna the best example o the boy's work, bit it wis still far abeen the craftsmanship o ony ither violin.'

'Three hunner thoosan? Fit boy?'

'At the Inverspaver Hotel. There wis a company up fae England. They'd hired the hotel ballroom and they were haein a sale o bankrupt stock. Ye ken, video-recorders for a fiver. TVs for a tenner. Sets o pans for 99p. What bargains there wis, Babbie. You and Virginia wid hiv been in yer element.'

'And you pickit up a Stradivarius violin amon aa this pans and TVs?'

'I couldna believe it masel. Ae minute I wis rakin through bales o sheets and winderin if there wid be ony holes in them, the next this young boy comes up and says I look like a man wi an eye for quality.'

'And you believed him?'

'He took me roon the back o a stand, kinna sleekit-like, and showed me this violin. I'll admit I wis worried the wye he wis aye lookin left and right, as if he didna wint tae be catched. I speired at him gin it wis a stolen violin, and he said no. It wis jist sic a bargain that if he announced it tae the crowd he wis feart there wid be a riot. He said he'd been lookin for a likely customer for days and he wis hopin I wis the man.'

Babbie lifted the violin. 'It disna feel affa hivvy,' she said.

'I said that tae the boy. He said it wis weel-kent that Stradivarius wis sic a craftsman that he wis able tae mak top-notch violins oot o the lichtest wid.'

'There's writin inside,' said Babbie. 'F.E.S.'

'I ken,' said Erchie, his eyes afire. 'That's fit maks it authentic. It stans for Fiolini Efabbricatore Stradivarius.'

Babbie peered a little harder. 'Hing on,' she said. 'There's mair writin farrer back. Get oot o ma licht.'

'Mair writin?' Erchie said. 'Fit dis it say?'

'I canna see. I'll get ma flashie.'

Babbie returned from the hallstand drawer with a little torch she kept for emergencies. She angled the beam inside the violin, while Erchie hottered about her, excited by this new development.

'It says,' Babbie said, grimacing as she peered. 'Oh, it's mair writin in front o yer F.E.S. There's three mair letters. Let me see. There's an F. There's a Y. And there's anither F.'

'I winder fit that stans for,' Erchie said.

'Babbie switched off her torch. 'F.Y.F.F.E.S.' she said. 'Fyffes.'

'Fyffes?' Erchie said. 'Fit could that mean?'

'It means yer fiddle's made oot o an aul banana box, Erchie.'

'What a craftsman,' Erchie said. 'He gets a top-notch three-hunner-thoosan poun violin oot o an aul banana box.'

'No, Erchie,' Babbie said. 'Ye're nae understannin, are ye? The only worthwhile fiddle here is fit the boy at the hotel did tae ye. Stradivarius nivver got a sniff o this fiddle. It's a knock-up tae fleece the public.'

'Nonsense,' Erchie said. 'It's got tae be a Stradivarius. I peyed £35.'

37 Fang, the Miracle Dog

SANDY Brose folded up his *Press and Journal* and whacked it down by the side of his seat in disgust. 'I dinna ken fit wye he keeps comin up here,' he shouted through to the kitchen. 'It's nae as if I've muckle time for him. Ye wid think he'd get the message that the trip fae Glesca's nae worth his while.'

'He must like ye,' shouted Geneva, elbow-deep among breakfast dishes in the sink. Then she muttered: 'Lord knows there hid tae be somebody.'

Sandy hauled himself out of his chair and shambled slowly through to the kitchen. 'Can we nae find an excuse or something? I ken he's ma cousin, bit . . .'

Geneva stopped the dishes and turned round. 'I dinna need an excuse,' she said. 'I've the kirk sale o work on Setterday aifterneen. It's you that needs the excuse. He's your cousin and it's you that he's comin aa the wye fae Glesca for.'

Sandy sighed and scratched his head. 'Could ye nae phone him and say I wis nae weel? Something smittin. The black death.'

'Sin ma soul? I'll dee nae sic thing. You winna tell ony lees eether. Ye'll tak yer medicine lik a man, and ye'll awa til Pittodrie wi him, lik he wints. He is yer femly, efter aa.'

'Ma Pittodrie days passed lang syne,' said Sandy.

'Dinna bother greetin here.'

'I'm mair an airmcheir fitba man noo.'

'I'm nae interestit.'

'It'll be caul.'

'I'm busy amon dishes. Awa and read yer paper.'

'He's affa roch and ready. Fowk stare and it gets embarrassin. Especially if he's got anither o his mangy dogs wi him, flechin itsel and piddlin.'

Geneva said nothing more and Sandy had little option but to shamble back to his chair by the fire and begin flicking idly through his *Press and Journal* again. 'Anither thing,' he muttered. 'He disna treat his pets affa weel. I canna be deein wi a man that bad-uses beasts.'

He looked up at the clock on the mantlepiece. It was already too late. Abbie, his Glasgow cousin, would have set off already.

THE spyocher, clatter and backfiring of a twenty-two-year-old Bedford Dormobile woke Sandy from his late-morning slumber. It took a few moments for him to come to himself, by which time Abbie, dressed in dungarees and being trailed by a four-legged animal of indeterminate breed, was half-way up the path to the front door.

Sandy glanced at the clock and hauled himself out of the chair intending to make a dash for the front door to lock it. Alas, his effort was in vain. By the time Sandy was out of the living-room and into the lobby, Abbie was through the front door and trailing his oily boots across Geneva's clean carpet.

'Sandy,' he said. 'Ye're aw set up fur the game, ur yez?'

'I can see you are,' said Sandy, eyeing the blue scarf, blue bunnet, blue rosette, blue semmit, blue socks and the G-E-R-S tattoos across the knuckles of both hands. 'Still supportin Celtic, eh?'

Abbie clapped him across the back and boomed a hearty laugh. 'Still crackin the jokes, eh? Listen, d'yez think we could tak your car. The Dormobile's no awfy great the day. It broke doon twice on the road up. Yez ur lucky I'm here ataw.'

Sandy sighed and said nothing, turning back towards the living-room.

'And hiv ye met Fang?'

Sandy stopped. A second later, Abbie stepped aside to reveal a small mongrel, scarcely bigger than a bag of sugar, sitting patiently behind its master and panting in such a way that it looked as if it might be smiling.

'There's nae muckle till't,' said Sandy.

'Size is no awthing,' said Abbie. 'This is a richt humdinger o a dog. Best I've hid and, as you ken, Sandy, I've hid a puckle dogs through ma hands in ma time.'

'Twinty at least, I'm sure.'

'Twinty-two.'

'Fit's sae great aboot him?'

'He's a Rangers supporter.'

Sandy studied the dog a little more closely. There was a blue rosette pinned to his collar but, that apart, there seemed to be little to distinguish him.

'He weers a rosette, ye mean?'

Abbie beamed. 'Better nor that,' he said. 'Huv yez a baw?'

'A ba?'

'A baw?'

'Oot in the shed.'

'Away and get it. We've twinty minutes spare. We'll drap in past the pleasure park on wir road and I'll show yez something yez winnae believe.'

SANDY huddled down into his anorak and hoped that no one he knew was looking. He needed a thorough psychiatric examination, he decided, having been sufficiently gullible to be lured to the pleasure park on a freezing spring day to watch a mongrel sporting a Rangers rosette and a grown man dressed like a Christmas tree chasing after an old beach ball.

'Ur yez waatchin?' shouted Abbie from the middle of the park. Sandy nodded and waved his arms to encourage his cousin to get cracking before someone sensible arrived.

'Awricht,' shouted Abbie. 'Waatch this.'

He squared up the ball at the centre circle while Fang sat patiently at the side of the goal. Abbie whistled what Sandy took to be an attmpt to sound like a ref's whistle for kickoff and began kicking the ball and jinking up the park as if tackling a multitude of opponents and beating every one. Sandy could feel the heat of embarrassment rising in him.

'And Rangers sco-o-o-o-ore,' Abbie shouted as he kicked the ball into the back of the net, then turned and ran a victory run, punching the air for the benefit of a crowd that was not there.

As Sandy watched, Fang rose on his hind legs and began tapping his front paws together. Abbie looked round and basked in Sandy's astonishment.

'Yez dinnae believe it, no?' he shouted as he picked up the ball.

'He's clappin his paws,' Sandy said.

'Dis that ivry time the Rangers score,' Abbie said. 'A brainy dog, Fang.'

132

Abbie began walking across and the little dog fell into a trot behind him.

'I hope ye're lookin efter a brainy dog like that better than ye did yer ither dogs,' Sandy said.

'This dog'll mak ma fortune,' Abbie said.

'Dis he dee onything fin ither teams score against Rangers?' Sandy said.

'Aye, he dis somersaults.'

'Somersaults? Foo mony?'

'Depends how far I kick him.'

38 Wayne Branded a Thief

FLO Spurtle put down the phone. She clenched her fists, closed her eyes and screamed a strained and frustrated: 'Aaaaaargh.' Hottering from one foot to the other, she was scarcely able to contain her rage, when Gibby opened the back door, home for lunch, and caught her.

He paused for a second or two, wondering if his wife habitually indulged in bizarre private habits or if she had just lost her marbles entirely. Flo stopped in mid-jig when she realised she was being watched.

'Aaricht petal?' said Gibby, in the over-light tone of someone who has witnessed a cataclysmic disaster and is trying to downplay it. He walked towards the sink.

'I've jist hid a phone call fae Mr Thole,' she said.

'The minister.'

'The minister.'

'Let me guess; he's needin an extra day's cleanin in the kirk hall afore the sale o work on Setterday.'

'Waur nor that.'

'Twa extra days?'

'It's a report back fae the Sunday School camp.'

Gibby reached for a towel and turned as he dried his hands.

'Wayne's been fechtin?'

'Waur nor that.'

'He's lost.'

Flo sat down at the table. 'Mr Thole wis affa nice aboot it. He said that they hidna come til ony conclusion yet, but he thocht it wis only richt that we kent.' She looked up. 'There's money missin fae Wayne's tent.'

Gibby paused for a moment, then began drying his hands again. 'So?' he said. 'Ye ken fit laddies is like. Wayne's maybe lost it. Or spent it.'

'It's nae Wayne's money,' said Flo. 'It's the ither laddie in the tent's money.'

'So the ither laddie's maybe spent it.'

'He says he hisna. They've askit Wayne aboot it and Mr Thole says Wayne canna come up wi an answer.'

Gibby sat down beside Flo. 'And is there muckle money involved?'

'Enough.'

'Foo muckle's enough?'

'Twinty-three poun.'

'Twinty-three poun?' Gibby stood up and began pacing round the kitchen. 'Fa lets a bairn awa til a camp wi twinty-three poun in his pooch? I hinna twinty-three poun in ma ain pooch.' He emptied his dungaree pockets as if to prove the point, revealing a tape measure, a small bag of flower ties and 53p in small change.

He sat down again. 'Are ye tellin me they think Wayne's a thief?'

Flo looked at him.

THEY took Wayne home two days early from the camp. Flo and Gibby went to collect him in their car, but they did not dally long. Mr Thole met them at the field gates and was anxious to impress upon them that inquiries were continuing and that under no circumstances had Wayne been identified as the guilty party.

He had even asked if they considered it wise to remove their son, given public impressions and how people talked, but Flo and Gibby insisted quietly that they thought it was for the best, and hoped that Mr Thole would quash any rumours until the facts were known.

The journey home was long and strained. Wayne said little. Flo and Gibby were bursting to ask questions, but could not bring themselves to do it in case they heard answers they did not want to hear.

Even when they arrived back at Stronach, Wayne had said not a word. He simply got out of the car with his little rucksack and went to his room where he began unpacking.

It was fully fifteen minutes before Gibby knocked at his door.

There was no reply, so Gibby knocked again, then opened the door a crack and peeped in. Wayne was lying, fully clothed, on the bed. He was staring at the ceiling, the back of his head resting on his hands.

'Wayne?' said Gibby. 'Can I come in?'

135

'Aye,' said Wayne. He spoke without looking at his father. Gibby walked to the side of the bed and sat down.

'Hiv ye onything ye should tell me?'

'No.'

'Are the stories true?'

'There's nae stories.'

'Did ye tak money that didna belong ti ye?'

'Div you think I did?'

'That's nae fit I asked ye. Did ye tak money that didna belong ti ye?'

Wayne looked at his father for the first time; a gaze of determination and defiance.

'I canna say.'

'If ye dinna say, fowk'll think ye did. They'll ca ye a thief. Naebody'll trust ye again. Ilky time they see ye, they'll be feelin for their purses and wallets, makkin sure they're still there. Ye'll get a reputation that'll stick wi ye the rest o yer days. Nae maitter foo muckle good ye dee noo and in the future; nae maitter if ye brak yer back raisin money for charities and helpin fowk for the hale o yer workin life, til yer dyin day ye'll be the laddie that stole twenty-three poun at the Sunday School camp.'

'It wisna twenty-three poun.'

It was not the answer Gibby had wanted to hear. 'So ye did tak money.'

'No, bit it wisna twenty-three poun.'

'Ye didna tak the money?'

'I canna say.'

Gibby sighed and ran his fingers through his hair. He paused for a moment.

'Wayne, whither it wis twenty-three poun, thirty-three poun, three poun or twenty-three pee, it wisna worth yer gweed name. Mair nor that, it wisna worth worryin yer mither for.'

Wayne looked back at the ceiling. 'Is she worried?'

'I think she's maybe doon the stairs greetin.'

Wayne looked back at his father.

'I'm sorry, bit I said I widna tell.'

'OK,' said Gibby. 'Ye've made a promise. I understand ye dinna brak a promise. Nae man braks a promise. So, let me see . . .'

He got up and began walking round the bedroom. Wayne's gaze followed him.

'Let's jist say for argyin's sake that this is a promise til anither loon.' He looked at Wayne for any sign of demur, but none came.

'And let's suppose this ither loon wis the loon that shared yer tent.' Still no disagreement.

'And let's suppose this ither loon wis feart o faivver took his money.' Wayne shook his head.

'No,' said Gibby, 'let's nae suppose he wis feart.' He thought for a moment, then: 'Let's suppose this ither loon ken fit happened ti the money.'

No disagreement.

'So let's suppose the money's nae lost or stolen.'

No disagreement.

'Bit . . . let's suppose the money's spent.'

Still no disagreement.

'Fit could it be spent on at a Sunday School camp?'

'A camp that's only half a mile fae the toy shop at Inverspaver,' said Wayne.

Gibby smiled. 'So let's suppose, this laddie bocht an expinsive toy and he's feart tae tell his femly, so he's said the money's missin and he's sworn his tentmate that he should keep the secret and the tentmate ends up lookin lik a thief because he winna brak a promise.'

Wayne smiled. 'I canna say,' he said.

Gibby sat down at the side of the bed and ruffled his son's hair. 'OK, I think we can sort this oot athoot you brakkin a promise,' he said. 'And I'm richt pleased that ye're nae a thief, for that wid hiv broken yer mither's hert.'

'I widna steal, dad,' said Wayne.

'No,' said Gibby. 'I dinna suppose ye wid. We've brocht ye up better nor that. Ye ken far bad loons that steal go.'

'Aye.'

'Far?'

'Woolies.'

39 *Thicker than Whisky*

THE hint of a stain in the bottom of Erchie Sotter's private glass at the Stronach Arms told a sad story. Erchie gazed at it disconsolately, then gazed round the empty bar.

'Ye're nae affa busy the nicht, John,' he observed.

'The weather,' said John, sorting through a crate of mixers and not looking up. 'An affa day o rain the day. Fowk are nae as hardy as they eest tae be. They're better pleased b'their ain firesides in front o the TV.'

'Nae affa sociable,' sniffed Erchie. 'A bittie rain nivver hurt onybody. Here am I, sivventy-sax, and I still manage doon the road.'

'The aul school, Erchie,' mused John, sliding the crate across to the back of the bar. 'Ye're een o the aul school.'

'Nae even Gibby oot the nicht,' said Erchie, looking round as if there might have been a chance that Gibby Spurtle had crept in unnoticed. 'It taks rale coorse wither afore Gibby disna look in by.'

'I dinna think it's the wither wi Gibby,' said John. 'I saw him doon the village at dennertime. He wis roon by the blood-transfusion mob up at the school. He said he didna like needles, bit he thocht it wis the least he could dee; gie a pint. He's likely at hame noo, collapsed. Ye ken foo big a bairn he is.'

'Affa public-spirited o him, lettin aff a pint,' said Erchie, 'bit it's the ither kinna pint he could hiv let aff in my direction gin he'd been here.' Erchie gazed sadly into his empty glass again.

'Of coorse,' said John, 'ye could aye buy *yersel* a drink.'

Erchie fixed John with a stare. 'Buy masel a drink?' he said, aghast. 'Buy *masel* a drink? Wi ma ain siller? Me, a pensioner?' He sat back on his stool and tugged at his collar, as if the very thought of spending his own money had overheated him.

That was when the swing doors opened and in walked Gibby, looking a touch on the pale side, but with no apparent ill-effects after his encounter with the blood-donor's needle.

'I'll hae a wee Maccie, John,' he said, placing both hands on the bar, as if supporting himself.

Erchie coughed.

'Aye, Erchie,' said Gibby by way of acknowledgement.

'Ye got on aaricht at the bleed fowk,' said John, putting a tumbler up to the optic.

'Weel, I'm still in ae bit,' said Gibby. 'I didna feel a thing at the time. I still dinna feel onything noo, though I've still got this bit plaster on ma airm. Bit I got hame and I'd ma tea and then I sat doon on the sofa and I jist got thinkin aboot the needle gaun in, burstin throwe ma skin and teerin intae ma flesh and the thocht jist conniched me aathegither.'

Erchie coughed again and slid his glass gently back and forth across the bartop in front of him.

'Aye, Erchie,' said Gibby turning towards him. 'Jist conniched.'

'So ye come oot for a breath o fresh,' said John, handing the whisky to Gibby.

'No, I come oot for a drink,' said Gibby. 'I couldna hiv sat in the hoose muckle langer. I wis pacin up and doon for a filie. I couldna settle. Then I telt Flo I needit something ti steady ma nerves.'

'I'm real nervous masel,' said Erchie.

'So she let ye aff the rope for the nicht,' said John.

Gibby took a sip of the whisky, then took a deep, satisfying breath. 'A free agent,' he said. 'It's real weet ootside the nicht.'

'Mair than it is in the boddim o this gless,' said Erchie, staring sadly at the bartop.

'Gie the loon a Grouse and shut him up,' said Gibby, fumbling in his pocket for more change.

Erchie perked up at once. 'There's nae need,' he said, then added hastily, 'bit I winna offend yer hospitality.' John took Erchie's glass. Erchie, meanwhile, turned towards his benefactor.

'Thank ye kindly,' he said.

'Dinna mention it, Erchie,' said Gibby. 'It's usually the invalid that gets bocht drinks, bit I suppose I should ken ye better or noo.'

'Are ye sayin I dinna stan ma haun?' said Erchie.

'In a nutshell, aye.'

'It's nae that I'm grippy,' said Erchie. 'I'm economical.'

'That's ae word for it.'

'And I'm a pensioner,' said Erchie, 'and pensioners is nae as flush as they can fling siller awye aa the time.'

'Jist noo and again wid be acceptable,' said Gibby.

'Ye widna hae a war hero buyin drinks for a young lad lik yersel ilky nicht, noo?' implored Erchie.

'I did think that ye micht mak a gesture the nicht,' said Gibby, 'me bein a bit o a hero masel, giein bleed.'

'Giein bleed. Giein bleed,' sniffed Erchie. 'There's fowk deein that daily-day. Michty, I'm on special call masel; me haein a rare bleed group.'

'They dinna tak fowk your age,' said Gibby.

'I'm a special case,' said Erchie. 'Ivver since I saved the life o the king o the Ogavambo tribe in the German Congo durin the war.'

'Nae mair waar stories,' sighed John.

'He wis affa poorly, the king,' said Erchie. 'And his doctors wisna makkin nithing o't. Then wir ain MO did a bleed test and discovered the king wis group X, the same as masel, so they hookit me up til him wi a bit rubber tube aff a half-track and wi baith lay back on the bed, side by side, for half an oor.'

'And did it work?' said John.

'I wyte it workit,' said Erchie. 'He wis up and aboot lik a young thing nae meenits efter they'd taen awa the tube. And what grateful. He shook ma haun and flung an airm roon ma shooder and he beamed intil ma face wi his great moofae o white teeth and he gave me a widden box. And fit wis inside the box? Three great big diamonds? "For you, Jock," he says. Weel, I took them, of coorse, because ye dinna like offendin kings, div ye?

'Nae twa days later, he'd a relapse, so the MO cried me ower again and hookit me up and lay me doon and the king got anither fill-up fae me.'

'And ye got anither three diamonds?' said Gibby.

'No,' said Erchie. 'This time, I got ae diamond.'

'*Ae* diamond?' said John.

'Ae diamond,' said Erchie. 'Weel, I wisna offendit, because I'd nivver really socht onything, onywye. I jist thinkit him kindly and put the ae diamond in wi ma three ither diamonds. Michty, nae twa days efter that, the king hid anither relapse and I wis hookit up again. It wis becomin a reglar thing, like.'

'And fit did ye get this time?' said Gibby.

'Weel,' said John, 'seein as he'd been pumpit fu wi Erchie's ain bleed by this time, it hid likely been a thank-ye note.'

40 *Babbie on the Bus*

BABBIE Girn slammed shut the door of the Inverspaver travel agent and turned to face the bustle on the street. 'Weel,' she said, harumphing and pulling her coat closer about her, 'that wis a waste o time, and nae mistake. Nithing atween yon deemie's lugs bit win.'

'Now, now, Babbie,' soothed Virginia, 'the lassie said hersel she wis jist startin, and aabody maun learn. We canna aa be expert in wir first wikk. And it is a new shoppie, efter aa. Gie them a chunce.'

'Gie them a month and they'll be shut,' said Babbie, scanning the street up and down. 'There's naebody'll trust their hol'days til a place lik that. Michty, fowk wid be landin here, there and aawye.'

'Fit aboot us landin a cuppie ower at the tearooms?' said Virginia. 'We can maybe work oot a new strategy ower a scone and jam.'

BABBIE stirred her tea with what she imagined was suitable fury. 'The trouble nooadays is that fowk dinna care aboot the customer. Ye dinna get the same personal touch. Shop assistants dinna ken their place. The customer's always richt. Bit some o that young fowk think they're airchie. Gie them a uniform and a badge wi their name on't and ye get nithing bit a hillock o chikk. Now, in oor day . . .'

'In oor day, we didna hae travel agents, Babbie,' said Virginia. 'In oor day, we didna hae travel. In oor day, we'd the Sunday School picnic and we lookit forrit til't aa year. We nae mair thocht o hol'days than flee in the air, and weel ye ken't.'

'I'm nae jist spikkin aboot travel agents,' said Babbie, clattering the teaspoon on the table. 'It's aabody. Young lassies at the end o the phone. Scaffies. Paper loons. Bus drivers. They're aa the same.' She took a first slurp of her tea, then added: 'I blame the TV.'

'They canna aa be the same, Babbie,' said Virginia. 'Aabody's different. I meet some rare young fowk. Fit aboot that young laddie drivin the bus doon fae Stronach? He wis affa helpful. A takkin kine o a loon. He even said he couldna believe ye wis a pinsioner wi a bus pass, and you sixty-eicht.'

'That wisna a compliment,' said Babbie. 'That wis jist mair chikk. He kent fine I wis a pinsioner. He wis jist rubbin it in. There's only ae gweed thing aboot that young bus driver; he's nae as chikky as the auler een. Thon auler lad's been needin a clap in the lugs for a while. If there's some wye tae get a body's dander up, thon chiel'll find it. He's ower sharp for his ain good.'

'Bit you can weel handle fowk lik that, Babbie. You're as sharp as ony o them.'

'Bit ye shouldna hae til. That's ma pint. A customer should be gettin the best o service. We pey sweetly eneuch for't. I dinna pey aa that money and expect a hillock o chikk in return. Naebody should.'

'It's jist banter,' said Virginia.

'Banter ma backside,' said Babbie.

'Weel, weel,' sighed Virginia, 'it's chikk. You win. Now, fit aboot this hol'day?'

'This scone's as hard as Henderson's,' said Babbie.

THEY wandered round a few of Inverspaver's shops, but with little heart. They would have taken the 3.20 bus back to Stronach but for Babbie's insistence that they get value for money from their bus passes. Consequently, they spent the last forty minutes sitting on the wooden bench at the bus shelter in front of the Central Church, staring emptily at the traffic as they waited for the 5.30 bus.

It was Babbie who broke the silence as the bus hove in sight. 'Dash it, dash it, dash it,' she muttered. 'Look fa it is.'

Virginia peered as the bus approached slowly and saw that it was being piloted by Babbie's bête noir, the older bus driver.

'Now, Babbie,' she said, gathering her few purchases and standing up. 'Dinna fash yersel. Ye've been workit up aa day. Let me get on first and I'll sort him oot.'

Virginia took up a strategic position right on the edge of the kerb, her back square to Babbie, and waited for the bus to slow.

The door hissed open and the driver looked down.

'Good afternoon, driver,' said Virginia, hauling herself aboard. 'Ye're in good time the day. It's richt fine tae see somebody cares as muckle aboot his job.'

The driver, mesmerised for a moment, smiled a wan smile of half-agreement, half-bewilderment. He barely looked at Virginia's pass as she manoeuvred herself into the seat by the door.

Babbie's progress up the steps was less elegant. She puffed and peched her way up the steps before ramming her pass under the driver's nose and glaring at him.

'Mak yersel comfy, ma dear,' he said. 'I winna start til ye're settled. We canna hae ye faain ower now, can we?'

As Babbie settled herself beside Virginia, Virginia beamed at her. The beam said: 'I told you so.'

They reached the outskirts of Inverspaver before Babbie spoke. 'It winna laist,' she said. 'He's likely been on some customer-relations course. Tak it fae me, a tiger disna change his spots.'

'Nonsense,' said Virginia. 'If ye're nice tae fowk, they'll be nice back. Dee as you would be deen til back, that's aye been my motto. Now settle doon and enjoy yer run.'

So the two chums chatted away for a few moments until Babbie glanced round and scowled.

'Fit's wrang, Babbie?' said Virginia.

'Hey, min,' shouted Babbie, leaning forward to bark at the driver, 'ye're awa the wrang road.'

'Nivver a wrang road,' said the driver without looking back. 'I've been drivin buses aa roon the North-east this last twinty-five year. I ken the roads lik the back o ma haun.'

'The road til Stronach's twa mile back the wye.'

'I ken that.'

'So ye missed it. We're on the road til Aiberdeen.'

'That's because this bus is gaun til Aiberdeen.'

Babbie sat forward sharply. 'Indeed, it is not,' she said. 'It's gaun til Stronach.'

'Weel, I'm sorry, wifie,' said the driver, 'bit seein as I'm drivin and you're nae, tak it fae me that this bus is headin for The Toon.'

'Dinna you get chikky wi me, mannie. We're nae needin The Toon. We're needin hame. And this is the Stronach bus.'

'It's nae the Stronach bus,' said the driver. 'It's the Aiberdeen bus. Ye said yersel it wis early. That's because it wis the 5.25 Aiberdeen bus, nae the 5.30 for Stronach.'

'Bit it said Stronach on the front o the bus. We baith saw it.'

'That's because the destination boord's broken,' said the driver, 'bit ony gype kens the 5.25's the Aiberdeen bus.'

'Listen, mannie,' said Babbie, 'if it says Stronach on the front, it should be gaun tae Stronach.'

'And listen, wifie,' said the driver, 'it says India on the tyres, but we're nae awa tae Bombay.'

41 *Godfrey Plays a Round*

INVERSPAVER Golf Course wasn't the most accommodating eighteen holes Godfrey Barrington-Graham had come across. He stood on the first tee, peering against a low February-morning sun, and quite unsure of how to play the ball.

He stepped back and turned to one of his playing partners. 'I'm most dreadfully sorry, Giles,' he said, 'but despite this course's proximity to our house, I'm afraid I'm thoroughly unfamiliar with it.'

'Think nothing of it, old boy,' said the portly, balding gentleman who was looking back at the clubhouse as he spoke. 'You keep harping on and on about it. Piers and I will begin to think you're something of a hustler.'

'Nothing hustling about it, I'm afraid. I'd guess that I have played this course not more than half a dozen times in the ten years we've been up here.'

'There's not a tame local who could help?'

'Not that I know. I'm afraid we don't keep much in touch with the locals back at Stronach. Well, Katherine sits on all manner of committees; you know what she's like. And I know even fewer people at Inverspaver.'

The door of the clubhouse squeaked open and a gangling man shambled out, sporting a pair of plus-fours whose check was so loud they might have benefited from volume control. He wore a fluorescent-lemon pullover and a floppy St Andrews bonnet with a red pom-pom planted square in the middle.

'You can't accuse Piers of not playing the part,' muttered Giles, 'but who's that little fellow with him?'

Godfrey looked up. 'Can't quite see,' he said. 'The sun off the clubhouse glass is a little dazzling.'

'Funny little chap,' said Giles. 'A bit like the tubby fellow who used to advertise cakes on the television.'

Godfrey held up a hand to block out the dazzle. At once, a pallor settled about him. 'Please, God,' he said. 'No.'

Piers strode up to the first tee. 'I say, what a stroke of luck, chaps. I happened to mention in the tinkler that we were a bit lost, the three of us, and that we'd hoped to find someone familiar with the course. And what do you know? This kind gentleman has agreed to give us three hours from his busy Sunday morning as a sort of ad hoc club professional. Dame Fortune has smiled upon us today; yes, indeed. Godfrey Barrington-Graham, Giles Cavendish-Frome, may I introduce Mr . . . ?'

'Sotter. Archibald Sotter,' said Erchie, stepping forward to shake hands.

'W-well, we thank you very kindly for the offer, Mr Sotter,' said Godfrey, 'but we could not dream of occupying so much of your valuable time. I'm sure we'll muddle through. Thank you, anyway. We won't keep you.'

'Ye've peyed me noo,' said Erchie. 'I'd be as weel's take a tekkie roon wi ye.'

'You've been paid?' said Godfrey.

'Thirty pounds was all he asked,' said Piers. 'Can you believe it? A man who played in the 1948 Open and we're getting his services for £30. We'll settle up later. Now, Mr Sotter, what would you advise for the first tee?'

While Erchie set about counselling Piers, Godfrey drew Giles to one side. 'Listen,' he muttered. 'I know this fellow. He's a jinx. Nothing good will come of this morning, believe me. If you value your hide, leave now. I beg you.'

Giles grinned. 'You sound like one of those housekeepers in an old horror movie, Godfrey. Look at Mr Sotter. He's a harmless old codger. Let's just enjoy the morning, shall we?' Giles strode back to where Piers was making minor final adjustments to his stance. And then . . .

WHACK!

'Oh, good shot, old boy. Good shot. Straight down the middle.'

Piers turned to Erchie and shook his hand. 'Mr Sotter, I salute you. I can see this is going to be the best £30 I've spent.'

Erchie peered down the fairway to where the ball lay and tried hard to conceal his shock.

*　　*　　*

SO the morning progressed with so few mishaps that even Godfrey Barrington-Graham permitted himself to breathe a little more easily. The further into the round, the more Giles and Piers became intent on advice which Erchie was more or less making up as he went along.

'Feet farrer oot, Mr Cavendish,' said Erchie, tapping the insides of Giles' shins with a stick he had picked up in the rough on the eleventh. 'Ye'll find that wi yer feet farrer oot ye get a smoother swing. No, no, nae grippin like that. Tak a ticht haud. Baith hauns on top o een anither. That's it. That's the boys. Noo, jist let yark in yer ain time.'

'He breaks all the rules,' muttered Piers to Godfrey, 'but, my goodness, it works. I've never had such a card in forty years of golf.'

'I can't believe it myself,' said Godfrey.

'Weel deen, yersel,' said Erchie, clapping Giles on the back. 'That's gweed twenty yards farrer nor I thocht. Come on, noo, Mr Barrington-Graham. It's your shottie.'

Godfrey stepped up to the tee. Trying to copy Giles' stance, he drew Erchie close and whispered. 'I don't know how you're doing it, Mr Sotter but, mark my words, if anything goes wrong now I'll have you strung up. Two important contracts are riding on this, and I don't want these people made to look fools. More than that, I don't want me to look a fool.'

'Mr Barrington-Graham,' said Erchie. 'Jist look at them. They're as pleased as pigs in a midden. Yer contracts is safe. Awa and hit yer ba.'

WHACK!

The ball sailed up and curved gently to the right. Four pairs of eyes followed it as it sailed towards the main Aberdeen–Inverspaver road. It bounced off a van windscreen. The van swerved into a layby, where it collided with a concrete rubbish bin. The jolt made the van's rear doors fly open and fourteen gross of oranges began spilling across the tarmac.

As Godfrey, Piers, Giles and Erchie watched, a cycle race arrived and, unschooled in manoeuvring through citrus fruit, the riders began tumbling into each other and onto the roadway. A car-driver realised that he was about to collide with thirty racing cycles and cyclists and jerked the steering-wheel hard to the right and up a farm road, where a trailerful of hay bales had been left. The bales spilled over the cars bonnet, revealing a courting couple who had been canoodling quietly. They slid gracefully down the hay and ended head-first in a sharny ditch.

'Oh, heavens!' said Godfrey. 'Oh, heavens. Oh, my goodness. What a calamity! Oh, my word! What on earth should I do?'

'Weel,' said Erchie. 'Try pittin yer hands a bittie farrer doon the shaft next time.'

42 *Up the Aisle*

THE outing with Bopsy-Wopsy, the village dog, to the new Waterside Park at Stronach appeared to have rekindled the dying embers of romance between Floretta Brose and Sammy Dreep. At any rate, Geneva Brose couldn't remember seeing her daughter so chirpy around the house in ages.

Over at the Dreeps', Walter and Aggie noticed that Sammy appeared to be substantially cheerier, too; offering to help in the kitchen and volunteering to wash the car, which until then had been unprecedented.

When he appeared in the kitchen for the final bucket of water, Walter drew him to one side. 'I ken fit ye're up til,' he said.

Sammy stopped. 'Fit I'm up til?'

'Ye're washin the car because ye're needin a shottie.'

Sammy flushed. 'It wid be affa handy,' he conceded.

'Floretta?' said Walter.

'Could be.'

'The pictures?'

'Maybe.'

'You tak the car wi my blessin,' said Walter, patting his son on the shoulder. 'It's important that ye're able tae get oot and aboot withoot worryin aboot fit ither fowk think.'

'Thanks, dad.'

'Jist ae thing. Dinna tell yer mither.'

Over at the Brose household, Geneva had left to go shopping down the village, leaving Sandy at home with his *Press and Journal* opened, as was his Saturday-morning custom, at the racing pages. Floretta, meanwhile, was doing the dishes and was humming bright little tunes to herself.

'Somebody's surely affa kittled wi themsels,' Sandy called from the living-room. His daughter appeared the the kitchen door, her rubber-gloved hands still foamy.

'Somebody's maybe got something tae be kittled aboot,' she said.

'Ye canna fool an aul sojer like me,' said Sandy. 'Ca it masculine intuition, bit I think ye've landit a new job. Am I richt?'

'I'm gaun oot wi Sammy the nicht,' said Floretta. 'The pictures at Inverspaver.'

Sandy beamed. 'So young romance is alive and weel and bidin at Stronach, is it?'

Floretta just smiled.

'We'll be hearin weddin bells afore lang, I doot,' he said. 'Ye'll mak a bonnie bride.' He put his arm round his daughter's waist and squeezed.

'Now, Mr Brose,' she said, walking back to the kitchen sink. 'Let's nae rin afore we're walkin. We've been doon this road half a dizzen times afore. Dinna build up ony hopes, because I'm certainly nae. I've learned better.'

'Bit I've a feelin this time's the richt time,' said Sandy. 'Sammy seems tae be settlin doon. He's nae dreamin daydreams nooadays. He's applyin for jobs, and wi his brains he'll easy get something. Na, I think yer wind's set fair, and nae mistake.'

'We'll see,' said Floretta. 'I've been through mair ups and doons wi Sammy than E&Ms lift manages in a wikk.'

Sandy pulled out a chair and sat down at the kitchen table. 'There's nae sic thing as wasted experience,' he said. 'Even fit seems tae be bad at the time, turns oot eesefae at some time. Maybe months or years later, bit mark my words; nithing's wastit.

'Here's you nae lang in yer twenties, nivver been mairriet, and I bet you ken things aboot the difficulties o romance that half the mairriet couples in the village disna ken. Ye've been throwe the mill, lass, and it's made ye a lot hardier, I wyte.'

'Maybe,' said Floretta. 'Although maybe I've jist hid good role models.'

'Yer mither and me?' said Sandy. He laughed. 'If only ye kent,' he said. 'Ye think you and Sammy's hid yer troubles wi yer on–aff engagement? Ye should hiv seen us thirty year ago. Oor coortin wis the spik o the place. And that's fit maks it aa the mair pleasin that you and Sammy's nae makkin oor mistakes.'

Floretta pulled off the rubber gloves and turned round to study her father. 'Mistakes?'

'Mistakes. Jist the little things that upset coortin couples. Ye ken how aathing's magnified fin ye're young. Well, fin ye're young and ye're Geneva, aathing's magnified and then magnified again. It's nae easy.'

'Tell me mair, Mr Brose.'

'Nithing tae tell. We got engaged in the September and fixed the weddin for the follyin June. Then during the Christmas and New Year in atween, een o ma aul girlfriends came back fae her job in Glasgow and yer mither wis convinced that we'd taen up wi een anither again.'

'And hid ye?'

Sandy managed a mock look of hurt. 'I certainly hid not. I wis formally engaged. I'm maybe a rogue, bit I'm nae a rat.

'I tried tellin yer mither that, bit what a persuadin it took tae mak her see sense. Her hale faimly wis efter me. I'd tae lie low for a wikk or twa til the heat went oot o them. Ye ken yer grandfather wis quick tae fire up wi his temper. And yer twa uncles, tee.'

'Bit it came aaricht again?'

'Come time. Come time. The lassie went back Doon Sooth efter New Year. Yer mither calmed doon and we wis hunky-dory nae lang efter that.'

'So ye'd plain sailin for the next five month afore the weddin.'

'I didna say that. Three wikks afore the weddin, this parcel arrives fae Glasgow. My big mistake wis thinkin it wis a weddin present for the twa o's so I took it roon tae yer mither's hoose tae open it.

'Oot came a pair o patterned long johns and a card that said: 'To My Great Big Sojer Boy. Keep Yourself Warm at Nights.'

'I didna ken far tae look. Yer mither ran greetin til her room. Yer grandmither glowered at me and flung the long johns in ma face. It wis a good job there wis neen o the menfowk in the hoose, or I'd hiv been flattened.

'I got up and left. Nithing I could say wid better the situation, so I jist rowed up the long johns back in their parcel and walkit oot. I thocht the hale engagement thing wis finished at that moment. I wis sure the weddin wis aff.'

'So fit put it richt?'

'Walter Dreep got a message fae een o yer uncles that the faimly wid like tae discuss matters wi me man tae man. They didna wint ony mair gossip in the village. They didna like tae think fowk wis lachin ahen their backs. They winted tae clear the air.

'I said I wis sorry if they'd got the wrang impression, bit it wisna my deein. I said it wis the lassie's idea o a little joke. If I'd kent fit wis in the parcel, I said, did they think I wid hiv come roon by their hoose tae open it in front o them and embarrass masel?

'I think yer grandmither began tae see sense first. Ye aye ken fin a North-east woman's beginnin tae see sense; she gies awa and pits on the kettle.'

'So aathing wis richt as rain?'

'Yer grandfather said he wis sure the parcel wisna my fault, bit he wis still worried that something wis goin on wi the ither lassie if she wis prepared tae spend money on anither woman's fiancy like that. He said he wisna prepared to wed his dother tae somebody that wis even hintin at takkin up anither lassie.'

'I said there wis nae chunce o that, because there wis naebody like Geneva.'

'So they left it at that?'

'Mair or less. We'd a frank exchange o views, ye micht say. Onywye, we shouldna be spikkin aboot the past. We should be spikkin aboot the future. It's you that should be the centre o attention noo.'

Floretta just smiled. 'And ye think Sammy and me'll be OK this time?'

Sandy stood and put his hands on his daughter's shoulders. 'I ken fine ye will,' he said. 'Unlike a lotta couples, ye're approachin this wi baith yer een wide open, aren't ye?'

Floretta shrugged and then nodded. 'I suppose so.'

'Exactly,' he said. And he pecked her lightly on the cheek. 'Unlike me, fa walkit up the aisle wi baith een closed.'

'Really?'

'Aye, her father closed ae ee, and her brithers closed the ither.'

43 *Sandy the Media Critic*

SANDY Brose had finished his Saturday tea; another fine repast of macaroni cheese and mashed potato, with a mug of tea to swill it down. He had then installed himself in the easy chair in front of the TV and had begun flicking through the channels.

It had taken him barely half a minute before he had tossed the remote control onto the sofa. 'Nithing worth a docken,' he said. 'Fowk's gettin paid good money for pittin oot trash like that. Ca themsels entertainers? They're a disgrace.'

Geneva appeared at the door from the kitchen, drying her hands. 'Did ye enjoy yer tea?'

'That wis rare. Filled a holie jist lovely. Did ye hear fit I wis sayin? I'm sayin there's nae a single programme worth watchin the nicht. Nithing bit Cilla Black and her spurtle legs or feel young laddies grinnin at the camera. That's nae entertainment.'

'Bit ye liked yer tea?'

'Lovely. Ye ken fine it's ma favourite.'

'That's good,' Geneva said, and she turned back into the kitchen.

'It's nae as if it's ony better at the picters,' Sandy called. 'Nithing bit violence, sweerin and punch-ups. If I wintit violence, sweerin and punch-ups, I'd jine the dominoes league doon at the pub.'

Geneva returned with the *Press and Journal*. 'Ye're maybe jist gettin aul,' she said.

'Gettin aul?' Sandy said. 'Because I dinna see onything entertaining aboot the trash they pit on the TV?'

'Your taste's maybe nae ither body's taste, though,' Geneva said. 'It wid be an affa borin world if we aa likit the same stuff.'

'Fit happened to the days o the classics?' Sandy said. 'Ye nivver hear o Z Cars noo, or Dixon o Dock Green, or Upstairs Downstairs. Now, that wis entertainment. Ye could sit doon in front o the TV and ken ye'd be entertained. Nae noo. Fit aboot quiz shows? Fit happened tae Double Yer Money or Criss Cross Quiz? They wis educatin and entertainin. Nae noo. It's aa greed noo. And the news? Ye nivver hear o Reggie Bosanquet or Andrew Gardner or Robert Dougall nooadays.'

'They're aa deid, Sandy.'

'That's nae excuse. They hid standards. Some o the new mob canna even tie a stracht tie.'

'Fit aboot a nicht oot at the theeter?' Geneva said.

Sandy turned in his seat and peered over his glasses at his wife.

'The theeter? In the toon?'

'Aye, the theeter in the toon. Plenty fowk dee that. Ging oot tae the theeter. Maybe stop in by somewye for a plate o mince and tatties on the road hame.'

'I'm nae gaun tae nae theeter. Hiv ye seen fit passes for entertainment in the theeter nooadays? Nithing bit pornography. Haulin the claes aff een anither. Settin a bad example. Ca that entertainment? Fin I think o the days o Harry Gordon and Will Starr and Larry Marshall, now that wis entertainment. Ye got a lach wi them. Ye could tap yer feet tae them. Half the fowk that gings tae the theeter nooadays are that sickened they jist aboot meet themsels comin oot.'

'I think ye're stretchin a bittie there. Fit aboot the radio?'

'The radio? The radio? Ye ca that entertainment? Thump-thump-thump music and a lotta silly yatter-chatter fae school laddies in American accents. Fit wye div they spik in American accents, onywye? Half o them wis brocht up in Torry.'

'I doot there's jist nae a please in ye the nicht,' Geneva said, and she disappeared behind her *Press and Journal*. 'It's a good job I gied ye yer favourite tea.'

Sandy paused. 'OK,' he said. 'Something's bein planned ahen ma back. Ye gie me ma favourite tea that ye only gie me if ye're saft-soapin. Then ye news me up aboot foo terrible the TV, the theeter and the radio is.'

Geneva slid the paper across to him. Sandy peered at the bottom of page fourteen. 'Reader offer,' he read. 'Cut oot a token a day for a month and get ten poun aff an excitin wikk's B&B at Strathdon. Subject to availability.'

'Nae that,' Geneva said. 'Lower doon.'

'For sale. Hardly-used pack of 23 horse-fertility pills. Taste of liquorice. £11.50 ono.'

'Nae that, eether. At the fit o the page.'

Sandy began reading then put down the paper again 'Not a chunce,' he said abruptly.

'No?'

'Ower my deid body. I hinna been at a circus since 1962. I didna enjoy it then, nae efter that accident wi the elephant and the syrup o figs larry. I'm nae gaun back. You please yersel, lady.'

'Ye'd enjoy it,' Geneva said. 'Aa the lichts and the glamour and the sparklin costumes. And it wid mean a lot tae me. The circus wis far we went on wir first nicht oot thegiether.'

'Anither reason nae tae ging back,' Sandy said. 'Circuses is aul hat. They're like music hall. Obsolete. Past it. Deid.'

'So ye're nae takkin me?'

'Correct. I'm nae takkin ye. I've nae mair a notion tae attend a circus than I wid rin doon the middle o the village wi nithing on. Excitin though that micht be.'

'Then ye're a selfish, selfish man,' Geneva said. 'Ye ken fine I like circuses. Ye ken they dinna come tae this pairt o the world affa often. There's een here next wikk and ye canna even dee me that little kindness. And efter me cookin ye yer favourite tea and aathing.'

'I'm a man o ma principles.'

'A man o principles? Dinna mak me lach. If ye wis even half a man ye wid tak me tae the circus.'

'If I wis half a man I wid be in the bloomin circus.'

44 Babbie's Mystery Callers

BABBIE Girn was standing at her kitchen sink, staring out at the back green as she waited for the kettle to boil, when the doorbell rang. She looked up at the wall clock, frowned, then shuffled towards the living-room door and on towards the lobby.

'Jist a minute,' she cried. She kicked back the coconut mat and slid two bolts.

Babbie opened the door and there, on the doorstep, stood . . .

. . . no one.

She stared for several seconds at the empty space where a caller was supposed to have been before she took a step outside and peered first up the Main Street and then down. A car was manoeuvring to park outside the chemist, but it was too far away. In the other direction, Walter Dreep appeared to be busy in his front garden, but Walter, too, was innocent simply by dint of distance.

Babbie stared at the doorstep again, as if it might hold some clue, then retreated inside and bolted the door.

She stood by the kettle for a minute or two more as it came to the boil. She sweeled a splash round the teapot, but was concentrating so heavily on her mystery caller that she began pouring the kettle of hot water down the sink. Almost half of it had gone by the time she came to herself.

'Och, dash ye,' she said aloud. Babbie paused for a second or two, then trotted through to the living-room. She chapped three times on the wall of the alcove and then scuttled through to the back door and outside.

A few seconds later, Virginia appeared at her own back door. Her hands were floury, for this was baking day.

'That's it again,' said Babbie.

'That's fit again?'

'Ma doorbell. That wis it again.'

'I didna see nithing.'

'Ye widna hiv seen onything, Virginia. Nae unless ye wis bakin wi yer nose against yer front windae. Did ye hear onything?'

'Not a thing.'

'Nae affa helpful, are ye?'

'Wid ye like a scone fin they're finished?'

'I'd like an answer til this doorbell business. That's the second day noo.'

Babbie worked over the doorbell mystery in her mind for the rest of the morning, all through her lunch of potted heid and a biled tattie, and into the early afternoon. Then, at last, she clapped her hands and smiled.

She hauled herself out of her easy chair and went through to the front door.

Once outside, she began ringing her own bell repeatedly, pausing to listen each time. So intent was she on her technical diagnostics that she failed to notice Erchie Sotter weaving his way home from the Stronach Arms. He stood for a moment to watch, then said: 'Are ye nae in, Babbie?'

Babbie looked round. 'It's ma bell. I think a connection's maybe lowse. It keeps ringin for nae reason.'

'For the past twa days?' said Erchie.

'Aye. Maist annoyin it is.'

'It's nae yer connections, Babbie; it's young loons fae the caravan site. I see them noo and again creepin up til yer door, pushin yer bell and rinnin awa.'

Babbie took a step or two down the path towards Erchie. 'Young loons?'

'Fae the caravan site. They're as fleet that they're ower the road, doon the slappie and awa intil the trees afore ye get til yer door. I think they must sit amon the trees and lach ilky time ye come oot.'

'*Thon* loons,' said Babbie. 'I gied them a moofae three days back for ricklin a stick doon ma palin and scrattin the pent.'

'There's yer answer. They're takkin revenge.'

Babbie scowled. 'Aye, we'll see aboot that.'

BABBIE sat behind her net curtains for several hours more that afternoon and early evening, but no young holidaymakers appeared.

She sat there for most of the next morning, and would have denied herself her mid-morning buttery and syrup had not Virginia arrived to relieve Mafeking with a plate of scones and jam.

'They've maybe tired o their game,' suggested Virginia.

'Nivver a tired,' said Babbie, munching a currant scone. 'That kinna fowk nivver tires o bein a nuisance.' She turned back to peer through the screens at the street outside and said, almost to herself: 'Bit they'll nae nuisance Babbie Girn and get aff wi't.'

The doorbell rang twice more in the next three days, and each time Babbie was too slow to get to the front door, although once she saw figures disappearing into the trees on the other side of the street and shouted: 'I'm phonin the bobbies!'

By the time Virginia turned up for their morning fly cup on the Friday morning, Babbie looked exhausted.

'I'm nae sleepin,' she told Virginia. 'Nonsense lik this maybe disna sound muckle, bit it fair taks it oot o ye. I'm nae as young as I eese'd tae be. I winder if this loons wid dee this kinna thing til their ain mithers?'

'Ye're nivver sure wi this kinna loons,' said Virginia. She looked at her friend, who was on the point of dozing.

'Virginia,' she told herself, 'we need a plan.'

THE following morning, they were almost ready. By the time they stepped back to look at their handiwork, which lay on Babbie's kitchen table, Babbie could feel her spirits rising.

'Now,' said Virginia, rinsing her hands under the tap, 'you tak that oot and set it on yer doorstep, and I'll awa up the road and be the lookoot.'

'And ye're sure ye can phone me in time?'

'As seen as I see them leavin the caravan site, I'll nip intil the phone box and gie ye twa rings.'

'And I'll nip oot the front and hide ahen the peenie rose.'

'And I,' said the male guest, 'will be ready for them.'

Virginia left a few seconds later. Babbie propped their home-made sign beside her polyanthus planter at the front door, then returned inside to her guest.

'Anither buttery?' she said. 'Mair tea?'

'No thank ye, Babbie,' he said. 'I'll nae get intil ma uniform if ye keep up this. Tell me, fit wye are ye sae sure this lads'll come this mornin?'

'Setterday mornin?' said Babbie. 'There's aye mischief in young loons on a Setterday mornin. I wid pit a fortnicht's pension on it. They'll be lyin stinkin in their beds until aboot half past ten, then they'll get up and think o some devilment, and I'll be their victim. I bet ye Virginia's on the phone afore the oor's oot.'

In fact, Virginia was phoning almost before the minute was out. The two rings, their coded signal, sent Babbie scuttling outside and down the ten yards to the front corner of her garden, where she crouched behind the peenie rose, her knees and ankles aching, and waited.

She did not have to wait long. The footsteps came a couple of minutes later. She heard them stop at her gate, then the sniggering began.

'Look at the sign,' she heard one Aberdonian adolescent voice say.

'Beware of the Budgie?' read another.

Then came stifled laughs and the squeak of the garden gate. Just as the doorbell rang, Babbie stood up. 'Can I help ye?' she said. She took three steps out on to her path and blocked the young man's escape.

He slid to a halt as quickly as his friend, who had been standing on the pavement, took off for the lane and the trees across the road.

'Far's yer killer budgie, than?' said the doorbell-ringer.

'It's nae a killer budgie,' said Babbie.

'Yer sign says Beware of the Budgie.'

'Exactly. It whistles.'

'Oh, I'm really scared. A whistlin budgie.'

Babbie looked over his shoulder to see her front door opening. There stood Sgt Alick Grip. The young man looked round and blanched.

'Sae ye should be,' said Babbie. 'This een whistles for the bobbies.'

45 *Wayne Wants a Puppy*

FLO put her hands on her hips and glared at Gibby. He was standing at the back door, which he kept half-open, clearly preparing her for a surprise. 'I'm warnin ye,' she said, 'if it's a new bike ye've wastit yer siller. Wayne canna keep a bike. I'll gie it twa month and it'll be scrattit and bashed tae ruination.'

'It's nae a bike,' beamed Gibby. 'Second guess.'

'I'm nae playin games, Gibby,' said Flo. 'I telt ye afore ye left this mornin that Wayne's birthday wis nae excuse for wastin siller, bit you insistit that ye'd met a blokie in the pub and fit he hid wid fair tickle Wayne's hert. Tickle awa, bit dinna expect ony interest fae me.'

'It's nae a bike,' said Gibby. 'Anither guess.'

'I'm nae haein toy guns in the hoose, eether. If ye've bocht him an airgun or nonsense lik that, ye can tak it straicht back and tell yer contact he can find somebody else for his stuff.'

'It's nae a weapon o ony sort,' said Gibby. 'Anither guess.'

'Weel, if ye've bocht him the pedal car ye nivver hid as a loon, ye've definitely wastit yer siller. He's ower aul for pedal cars. He's at an age far he wints a real Ferrari or a Porsche or a BMW. Ye ken that by the picters on his bedroom wa.'

'It's nae a bike. It's nae a gun. And it's nae a car,' said Gibby. 'Gie up?'

Flo sighed. 'Come on than, Paul Daniels, fit is't ye've got ahen yer back?'

'Jist a mintie,' said Gibby, and he stepped back outside the door. Flo heard him puffing and panting as he manoeuvred some bulky package from the bottom of the steps outside, up to the top.

As he manhandled the package inside, Flo saw that it was a cardboard box that had once contained boxes of breakfast cereal.

'A year's supply o cornflakes?' she said.

'Jist a mintie,' puffed Gibby as he squeezed it between the door-posts and teetered towards the kitchen table, where he laid it down.

'Now,' he said. 'Fit div ye think?'

Flo strolled round the box to where Gibby stood. Then she stopped and stared at the contents. The contents stared back at her. Then Flo turned to Gibby, her face set grim. 'Under no circumstances, Gilbert Spurtle,' she said. 'Tak that object back far it cam fae and leave it.'

'Flo, Flo, Flo,' soothed Gibby. 'It's exactly fit the loon needs. It'll learn him responsibility. He'll hae something else ti think aboot bar himsel.'

'He his nae sense o responsibility noo,' said Flo, 'and I canna see as a puppy'll cure him. I ken fine fit'll happen. Muggins here'll be left lookin efter't. The answer's no, Gibby. No. No. No.'

At which point Wayne burst in at the back door, about to clamour for his tea, when his gaze fell on the cardboard box, rudimentary home to an eight-week-old rudimentary puppy.

'A puppy,' he cried. He scooped up the little animal; held it up to his face so that it almost glowed in his excitement, then cradled it in his bosie and beamed up at his mother and father.

Gibby looked at Flo.

Flo pursed her lips and looked at the floor, then looked up again. 'Fit's it's name?'

'Roozer,' said Gibby.

'I micht hiv kent a gairdener wid pick a feel name lik Roozer. Is that because it wis born in a gairden shed?'

There was a gentle spattering sound off the kitchen vinyl, and a dark stain crept down the front of Wayne's school jersey.

'Nae exactly,' said Gibby.

Over the next few days, Wayne and Roozer became inseparable. They played on the back green in the mornings. They played on the back green in the afternoons. In the evenings, when the puppy was desperate to sleep, Wayne persuaded it that it was not really tired at all and wanted to play some more.

He was a dutiful owner. He brushed the little animal more than it really needed with an instrument that was far too big for it. He arranged the food in its bowl with far greater care than ever he arranged his own. He sat by it, conversing with it in far more animated terms than ever he conversed with his parents or his sister.

None of this went unnoticed by Flo or Gibby. They watched him from the kitchen window, amazed by the transformation in their son to such a degree.

'I think ye've maybe hid a good idea efter aa,' Flo told Gibby as they climbed into bed one evening. 'As lang as he sticks at it and the novelty disna weer aff and I'm nae left lookin efter a dog as weel as the three o you, I think he micht turn intil a richt conscientious kinna laddie as far as dogs is concerned.'

'Fit did I tell ye?' said Gibby, as if he had known all along. 'Lik faither like son.'

'You didna hae dogs as a loon,' said Flo.

'Indeed, I did. Well, it wisna sae muckle my dog as ma faither's, bit I got the job o lookin efter't, even although it wisna nivver really my dog, as ye wid say.'

'Yer faither hid a dog?'

'Fit's funny aboot that?'

'Your faither hid a dog? Aul Spurtle wis as roch a character as there's ivver been roon Stronach. Some wid even say he wis coorse. I canna see him ainin a doggie. Did it survive lang?'

'Ye've nivver hid an affa good word on ma faither,' said Gibby. 'I may tell ye that he thocht mair o that little doggie than ivver he thocht o ony o us.'

'He'd his priorities richt, than?'

'That little doggie wis treatit as weel as ma faither kent foo,' said Gibby. 'He wis chicken-hertit fin it come til animals.'

'He surely hid tae discipline it,' said Flo. 'Ye're nae tellin me he jist let a dog rin riot.'

'He used tae kick it here, there and aawye,' said Gibby, 'bit he aye took aff his tackety beets first.'

Flo laughed. 'We'd a dog wirsels eence,' she said. 'At least, the neebors did. A sassidge dog, he wis. A great lang thing. Affa low-slung. Ye aye felt richt sorry for him in the sna. Didna survive lang, though. It took a hert condition or something. Us kids wis nivver telt that, of coorse. The neebors tried tae be kind. They said it met its end walkin roon and roon a tree.'

'That wid be richt enough.'

Flo reached up and switched off the wall light, plumped up the pillows and settled back.

'We'll need tae start trainin lessons for Wayne and Roozer,' she said. 'Ye canna start early enough wi trainin a doggie.'

'And I ken the very man,' said Gibby.

'Nae Erchie Sotter.'

'Fa better? Erchie's a wizard wi dogs. Nae maitter foo young they are, they dee exactly fit he tells them.'

'Such as?'

'Mind fin Mr Thole the minister hid an alsatian? Erchie took it oot ontil the back green and telt it: 'Heel.' And that's fit it did.'

'Fit?' said Flo.

'It took a chunk oot o his heel.'

46 *Memories of the Flood*

THE newsreader's tones were suitably grave as the Spurtles sat, aghast, at the scenes of flood and devastation in Moray being played before them. Flo leaned forward in her seat and shook her head at TV shots of submerged cars, flooded streets and valiant attempts to deploy sandbags against the worst that heavy rain and high tide could do.

'Peer fowk,' she said. 'What an affa thing. Isn't that an affa thing, Gibby?'

'The reddin-up'll be waur,' said Gibby. 'It's nae as if flood watter's clean watter. It's fool, orra watter. I often think a flood must be as bad as a fire.'

Flo turned. 'Ye'd think ye'd personal experience.'

'I hiv,' said Gibby. 'The February o 1968 fin the Water o Stronach burst its banks and flooded the back eyn o the village. We'd nivver seen onything like it. Watter, watter ivrywhere and nae a drop for a drink. The fire brigade hidna the pumps tae cope. Fowk wis floatin doon the road for their pensions. We'd the reporters and the film crews roon aboot for twa days and then, efter aa the excitement wis by, aabody forgot aboot's: the cooncil, the press, the insurance companies, the government. That's fit wye the fowk ower Elgin wye maun keep timmerin up the authorities. Ye dinna get nithing if ye dinna shout for't nooadays.'

'I mind noo,' said Flo. 'Wis that nae the big flood efter it rained for near a fortnicht non-stop? Hale watter. Burns wis rivers and rivers wis lochs and lochs wis oceans. It nivver dauchelt fae the eyn o January til the start o July, if I mind richt.'

'That's richt,' said Gibby. 'And the cooncil wis affa put oot because they thocht they widna get tae apply their usual hosepipe ban. So they did it onywye.'

'Happy days,' sighed Flo.

'Erchie Sotter said the last time he'd seen as muckle watter as that wis in Ebenezer Grip's Hogmanay bottle,' Gibby said. He looked at his watch then hauled himself up from the sofa. 'In fact, Erchie'll be here in twa–three minties. We're awa til the bowlin-green.'

'Ye canna be bowlin wi the grun as weet as this.'

'Erchie disna let little thingies lik watter stop him.'

There was a cursory knock at the back door followed by footsteps.

'Ben here, Erchie,' cried Gibby, and presently the door from the kitchen opened and there stood Erchie, bowling bag in hand.

'Hullo aabdy,' he said. 'Oh, I see ye've the news on. Isn't it affa aboot the floodin ower by Elgin? That peer fowk. I widna be in their sheen for onything.'

'I wis jist mindin Flo on the floods thirty year ago roon aboot here.'

'They wisna as bad as this Elgin floods,' Erchie said, 'bit they wisna far ahen. It wis jist a great lang tragedy as far as I wis concerned.'

'Fit wis the tragedy?' Flo said. 'Drooned beasts? Ruined craps?'

'The cellar at the pub wis aneth nine fit o watter,' said Erchie. 'Ye couldna get a decent dram or pint for love nor money.'

'Aye,' said Gibby, 'that maun hiv been the warst flood ony o's his ivver experienced.'

'Na,' said Erchie. 'There wis a waur flood nor that, though you twa'll be far ower young tae ken onything aboot it. It wis nae lang efter the start o the waar.'

'I dinna mind ma fowks spikkin aboot a wartime flood,' said Flo.

'Nae in the village,' said Erchie. 'It wis oot at the back edge o the Vale, far the Water o Stronach and the Spaver Burn meet. Ye ken, that potchie bittie that's nae eese for nithing.'

'Far yer fowk fairmed?' said Gibby.

'Or tried til,' said Erchie. 'Nivver affa gweed grun at the best o times, bit it wis gey sair that eer, let me tell ye. Ma faither could mak nithing o't. It wis only thanks tae ma mither that we keepit body and sowel thegither. I think it wis aff her that I got ma indomitable outlook. Nivver say die, that wis oor motto.'

'Hid she a hard life, Erchie?' said Flo. 'I canna say's I mind on her ata.'

'Ye widna, lass. Ye widna,' said Erchie. 'Ee'd hiv been still in hippens fin she deed. Bit it's nae mony fowk can calve a coo at ninety-three.'

'Did she really?' said Flo.

'Nae in as mony wirds,' said Erchie. 'The coo rolled on tap o her and that wis the aul bird bladdit beyond repair. Bit div ye nae admire her spirit for tryin? I often think she'll be in a far better place aenoo, timmerin them up. If there's a Hivven, she'll be there wavin a poker and giein oot orders. Mair tae the pint, they'll be deein fit they're telt. Ye didna ignore my mither and get aff wi't.'

'Ye wis real fond o yer mither,' said Flo.

'I wis, lass. I wis,' said Erchie. 'Nae lang efter the waar broke oot, she took me til ae side and she said: "Erchie," she said. "This femly his nivver held back in a crisis. There's nae cooards in this hoose. There's a war on and I'm nae haein callin-up papers arrivin at this hoose and the hale village kennin that we didna volunteer." Then she jist glared at me wi ae ee and I kent exactly fit she meant.

'So that wis fit wye her and me come tae be stannin at the dockside at Rosyth three wikks later. Aa roon aboot me wis sweetherts bosiein intil een anither, sayin their goodbyes; the weemin roarin and greetin.

'Then there wis me and ma mither. Nae roarin and greetin wi us. We wisna that kinna femly. There wis nae public emotion amon the Sotters. We jist kinna stood there, facin een anither. Kinna aakward. Neether o's kent fit tae say, although we kent we widna see een anither for a file. In fact, we kent we maybe wid nivver see een anither again if things got really bad.

'So we jist stood there for a file, spikkin aboot the fairm and the nowt and aathing and then the time come for pairtin and boardin the cruiser, and we jist lookit at een anither and then she turned awa, and that wis that.'

'Oh, Erchie,' said Flo, sniffing. 'What an affa sad story. Ye must hiv been hertbroken deep inside.'

'I wis,' said Erchie. 'Bit I couldna show that tae ma mither. She wis a tyeuch aul bird, as ye say. She'd hiv been black-affrontit. I wid hiv let the side doon.'

'And ye nivver saw her again for twa year.'

'Weel,' said Erchie, 'I did catch a glimpse o her stannin on the deck as her boat slid oot o the herber.'

47 *Wayne's Romance Problem*

FLO Spurtle sat outside the door of the primary-school headmaster, waiting to be called for her appointment. She glanced at her watch and bit her lip, then cross-checked with the wall-clock behind the school secretary.

'Excuse me, Elsie,' she said. 'Is that the richt time?'

'Set it masel this mornin, Flo,' said Elsie. 'Aff the peeps on the radio. Ye canna get better.'

'Richt enough,' said Flo, sitting back and sighing.

'Ye're affa nervous-like,' said Elsie. 'I widna worry aboot it. There's fowk comin in here daily-day efter an invite fae the dominie. Sometimes he's jist needin a news.'

'We've been deein an affa newsin aboot Wayne since ivver he startit the school,' said Flo. 'This is the ninth or tenth time. It's nae affa relaxin.' She looked at her watch again. Elsie was about to offer Flo some coffee when the door opened and Wayne's teacher, Miss Pink, invited Flo inside.

Flo stood up, looked across at Elsie as if to say: 'Here goes', and Elsie smiled back at her.

THE headmaster cleared his throat. 'You'll be pleased to hear, Mrs Spurtle, that this is nothing major. It's just that, sometimes, if a teacher is especially diligent' – he looked across at Miss Pink, who blushed at the implied compliment – 'we sense that a problem is arising which is better dealt with sooner, not later.'

Flo nodded earnestly and, feeling that she had better say something to fill in the gap in the conversation, added: 'I could not agree with you mair. My Gibby and me, we're aye nipping problems in their buds.'

'Quite, quite. Well, perhaps if Miss Pink relates a little of the issue in hand, we can discuss how best to proceed. Miss Pink?'

Miss Pink leaned forward. 'The thing is, Mrs Spurtle,' she said in her customarily empathetic tones, 'for a week or two now, I have been growing a little more concerned about Wayne. You and I know that he has always been an active little boy, not to say a little butterfly-minded. It has always been harder for Wayne than most other children in his class to concentrate on his lessons. With the slightest distraction, he can be lost in a world of his own. Well, these last two weeks, even the modicum of concentration that he had has simply vanished.'

'Vanished?' said Flo.

'Gone. Disappeared. Nothing at all. He simply sits there blankly. He won't talk. He won't react. Even his friends are a little alarmed about him. And we simply wondered if has been like this at home.'

Flo thought for a moment. 'Noo that ye mention't,' she said, 'he his been affa doon aboot the moo, aye. We jist thocht it wis the end o the fitba season.'

'I don't think it can be that,' said the headmaster. 'Especially for a Dons supporter. He'd be glad to see the back of any season.' He chortled at his little joke, then composed himself. 'So,' he said, 'nothing wrong at home that you know of, but similar symptoms.'

'In which case,' said Miss Pink, 'I think now is the time to venture my little theory.'

THE back door opened and Flo looked up from stirring the cheese sauce for their macaroni tea. 'That's me hame,' said Gibby.

'And high time,' said Flo. 'Ye're nivver here in a crisis. Yer loon's in sic a state that I wis cried up for a meetin at the school. They're worried aboot him. Which is mair nor I can say for you.'

'Fit's adee?'

'He's in love.'

'He's fit?'

'He's in love. He's taen a shine til a lassie in his class and she's nae lookin the road o him.'

'He's only nine.'

'He's only nine and he's mopin and mollochin aboot because he's been hutten wi Cupid's arras.'

'Fa's the lassie?'

'They didna say. Wayne winna say. I canna tell ye. Awa ben and hae

169

a newsie wi him. You'll maybe get something – onything – oot o him and mak him see sense.'

Gibby glanced at his watch. 'I hinna lang,' he said. 'Erchie's comin roon in twenty minutes. We're awa bowlin the nicht.'

'Oh, I'm affa sorry troublin ye. Of coorse, bowls and Erchie Sotter's mair important then yer loon.'

On schedule, twenty minutes later, Erchie Sotter arrived at the back door. 'Come in, Erchie,' cried Flo.

Erchie stepped inside. 'Oh, fine smells,' he said. 'Ye're nae at yer tea, are ye? Far's the man?'

'Ben in the livin-room. We've a problem wi Wayne. He's in love.'

'Is that a problem?' said Erchie. 'He's a growin loon. The mysterious wyes o Aphrodite and her nymphs come til's aa.'

'Nae til a nine-year-aul.'

'If it's guidance in maitters o the hert ye're needin, I'm the very man. They didna ca me the Casanova Kisser o Calais for nithing. Ye dinna mind if I tak a tekkie ben?'

Before Flo could protest, Erchie had stepped into the living-room.

In less than a minute, Gibby was back in the kitchen, minus Erchie.

'Far is he?' said Flo.

'Ben haein a word wi Wayne. He suggestit I leave because he wis the man that could tell Wayne a thing or twa aboot weemin.'

Flo stuck her hands on her hips and scowled. 'And ye left a mannie lik that wi a nine-year-aul laddie? Yer ain loon?'

'I couldna get nithing oot o him. He jist sits there sulkin.'

'Ye think Erchie Sotter'll dee ony better?'

'He canna dee ony worse.'

Flo began to march towards the door, but Gibby stepped smartly in front of her. 'Jist leave them,' he said. 'Wayne's in een o his thrawn moods. Fa div ye think'll come aff best?'

Flo stopped, then smiled.

Gibby ate his tea, cold and leathery though it had become, then, conscious that time was slipping past for the bowling, he opened the living-room door and peeped in. There sat Wayne, in the same position as before, but now smiling up at Erchie.

'So ye see, Wayne,' Erchie was saying. 'Nae maitter foo big yer romantic problems, they'll nivver be as big as mine wis durin the waar. I mean, you'll nivver hae twa weemin fechtin a duel ower ye, will ye?'

'I dinna suppose,' said Wayne.

'That's ma loon,' said Erchie, ruffling Wayne's hair and standing up. 'Now, yer dad and me's awa bowlin. Keep yersel cheery and dinna gie't a second thocht.'

Erchie strolled from the living-room, beaming triumph. He collected his bowling things from the back doorstep, while Flo stared, agape, from Erchie to Gibby and back to Erchie.

As Gibby and Erchie walked along the side of the house, Gibby said: 'Erchie, that story's nae true, is it?'

'Fitna story?'

'The story aboot twa weemin fechtin a duel ower ye?'

'I wyte it's true. Twa French lassies in Normandy durin the advance efter D Day. They were that annoyed aboot the dual romance that they resorted tae guns tae sort it oot; tae see fa wid get me.'

'And fa got ye?'

'They baith did. Een in ma leg, the ither een in ma backside.'

48 *Dietary Nightmare*

THE ten-inch Christmas tree at the end of the bar and a solitary string of tinsel, draped in loops along the top, hardly inspired confidence that the festive spirit had arrived at the Stronach Arms.

The point was not lost on Walter Dreep and Sandy Brose, out for their first Thursday-evening tipple since the demise of Mother Dreep several weeks before.

'Ye're gey thin on the decorations, John,' observed Sandy. 'Hiv ye nae hid time, or are ye jist lik the rest o's – fed up wi Christmas?'

'Nae time,' said John. 'It was aa that I could dee tae get up that bit tinsel. Onywye, I wis a bittie sickened last year efter I put aa that effort intae pittin up a richt tree ower in the corner and naebody as muckle as lookit the road o't. I needna hiv bothered. So, this year, I hinna.'

'Fair dos,' said Walter, taking his first sip as he looked about him, 'although it disna dee muckle tae gie the bar that atmosphere o festive waarmth.'

'Nivver mind the festive waarmth, John,' said Sandy expansively and clapping his ample girth. 'It's mair a belly's waarmth that interests me. Man, I'm richt hungry. Hiv ye ony o yer mince-and-tattie pies left?'

John stepped to the back of the bar and brought out a large plastic plate covered by a clear-plastic dome, in the centre, among an array of crumbs and white, congealed lard, sat a sad, solitary pie.

'Last een, Sandy,' said John. 'Will I pit it in the microwave, or will ye hae't caul?'

'Microwave, if ye please,' said Sandy, fumbling in his pocket for change. 'I like the fat rollin doon ma chin. Oh, and I'll tak a cigar fan ye've a meenitie. I aye think ye need a cigar at Christmas.'

It took John a few moments to fulfil these Christmas wishes, but soon Sandy was duly furnished, drink in one hand, lit cigar in the other and a pie swimming gently in grease on a paper plate in front of him.

Which was rather an inappropriate moment for the bar door to swing open and a new customer to arrive.

'Michty,' said Sandy. 'It's nae aften we see yersel in here, doctor. Will ye tak a Christmas something?'

'I don't mind if I do, Mr Brose,' said the village GP, brushing a few flakes of snow from the shoulders of his Crombie coat as he walked towards the bar. 'I'll have a small whisky, if you don't mind.'

'A wee Maccie for the MO, John,' said Sandy, shoving some change across the bar. 'And fit's taen ye here the nicht, Doc?'

'Well, I just felt like it,' said the doctor. 'Heavens, I might be a doctor and I might be on call for nights on the trot, but it doesn't do to stick at home all the time, you know.'

'Good man,' said Sandy. John put the whisky in front of the doctor, who accepted it and raised his glass.

'Cheers,' he said.

A few moments later, he added: 'Mind you, Mr Brose, I'm a little alarmed at your lifestyle, if you don't mind me noticing. I don't want to talk shop, but you're not helping me at all.'

Sandy looked at the drink, the cigar and the greasy pie.

'A wee treat til masel, doctor,' he said. 'I dinna mak a habit o't.'

'I'm glad to hear it, for you're working yourself towards a calamity. Anyway, this is not the time for lectures. How are you all keeping?'

'Excuse me for speirin, doctor,' interrupted Walter, 'bit I've been haein an affa trouble shakkin aff this caul that I've got. Fit wid ye dee?'

The doctor smiled to himself, for this was precisely why he rationed his village socialising. Even when he was off duty, he was rarely off duty.

'Well, Mr Dreep,' he said, 'I'm going to tell you what you want to hear. I would prescribe a wee whisky and an early night. That's as good as anything.'

'I've aye said ye wis a richt gweed doctor,' boomed Sandy.

'I see,' said Walter. 'And fit aboot my wife, for I doot I've gien her the smit and it's intil her chest noo.'

'Well,' said the doctor. 'For a severe case I would probably prescribe two whiskies and an early night.'

'Bit she tried that,' said Walter. 'That wis near a wikk ago and it hisna workit ata.'

'In that case, I would increase the dose and try three whiskies.'

'And supposin that didna work, wid ye try fower whiskies?'

'I certainly would,' said the doctor, 'provided they were well spaced apart. A little of what you fancy for medicinal purposes never did anyone any harm.'

'A richt gweed doctor,' said Sandy knowingly to John.

'So ye're sayin that ye should keep increasin the dose until it works?' said Walter. 'Is that richt? I mean, could we get the length o eicht whiskies, for example?'

'If that was what it took and she wasn't suffering any other, shall we say, effects then, yes, I suppose you could go as far as eight whiskies.'

'Jist supposin, doctor,' said John, 'that the patient didna like whisky. Fit wid ye dee wi a patient lik that.'

'The patient didna like whisky,' smiled the doctor, sipping at his nip. 'Well, John, I suspect that's a patient not worth the curing.'

49 *Watchnight Woes*

THE Reverend Montgomery Thole was glancing through the order of service one last time when the village headmaster knocked twice and peeped round the door. The dull buzz from next door grew to a clamour. 'I think we're almost ready, Montgomery,' he said. 'Are you all set yourself?'

Mr Thole said: 'Indeed', as if he were about to begin on ordeal, not a service to herald the birth of Baby Jesus. The headmaster stepped into the vestry and closed the door behind him.

'Montgomery?' he said. 'Is everything all right? I've not seen you look this dejected before.'

'Och, I'm fine, Claude,' said Mr Thole. 'Just put it down to the wanderings of a man who is suddenly feeling his age.'

'I've never seen the church so full,' said the headmaster. He was scrabbling for some means of cheering up his friend. 'There are all sorts of people here whom we never see from one year's end to the next. Surely that lifts your spirits.'

Mr Thole put his papers back on the table. 'Well, Claude,' he said, 'if you must know, that's precisely what I find so dispiriting. I am, of course, more than delighted to welcome so many unfamiliar faces into church. We are achieving a great deal if we manage that, are we not? And there is always the chance – however remote – that some might get a taste for it and become recidivists in the best sense.'

The headmaster looked puzzled.

'But don't you see,' said Mr Thole, 'it's not the fact that they are here tonight; it's that they are not here any other night, or any other Sunday. How can I hope to have any bearing on these people's lives if I cannot have access to them?

'Och, I can't help blaming myself. I know all the standard discussions in presbytery about modern people's pressure of time and the busy lives everyone leads nowadays but, when you boil it down, the cold, hard truth is that if my sermons were interesting, uplifting and entertaining, people would find the time. They would fight to find the time to be sitting there every Sunday throughout the year. It has to be my fault, for it cannot be anyone else's. I would be fooling myself to pretend otherwise.'

The headmaster looked at his watch. 'Montgomery, I'm not sure that there is time for theological discussion at the moment. You have about 300 people through there . . .'

'Oh, I don't mean that I should be cracking jokes from the pulpit and doing card tricks between hymns, but I need to be a little better at holding their attention. I need to attune myself more to a younger audience, don't you think? A little more, what's the word, hippety-hip?'

'Well, that's one way of putting it perhaps,' said the headmaster. 'Now, don't you think you should go . . .'

'Do you know, Claude, I can tell just by scanning the faces that any normal kirk service is attended out of habit and duty, rather than desire. The ones I really want to get at are the people sitting just at the other side of the wall right now; the ones who would no more think of coming to church on a Sunday than they would think of going to the North Pole for their summer holidays. But how to do it? How to do it?'

'Montgomery, I . . .'

'I can always tell how well a service has gone just by looking at Mr Grip from the shop. He has attended more church services in nearly a hundred years than I have conducted during my entire career. If Mr Grip is still awake, I know I'm doing well. If he manages to say something remotely friendly at the door afterwards, it's one of my all-time best.'

The headmaster grasped Mr Thole's arm and led him towards the door. 'Well, you'll be pleased to hear that Mr Grip is sitting there as usual, third row back, second seat in from the left, and he looks in very good spirits, so that's you off to a flying start. Now, get yourself ready because you have 300 people anxious to be sent home uplifted in time for Christmas Day.'

'Ah, Christmas Day, that modern festival of conspicuous consumption. That Mammonite orgy of materialism and greed. Of course, we must prepare them for that. Up and at them, Claude, eh?'

The headmaster paused. 'Look, Montgomery,' he said, 'are you doing anything for Christmas Day? You seem to need your spirits lifting. You need something to look forward to if you're to have any hope of delivering the uplifting service you seem to want to deliver. I know how lonely it must be for a single person while everything on the day is geared to family. So Clarice and I would be delighted to have you as our guest.'

Mr Thole clapped the headmaster's forearm. 'I thank you kindly for such a kind gesture, Claude,' he said, 'but I'm having my cousin Mina from Banchory for lunch on Christmas Day.'

The headmaster stepped aside and opened the door.

'I'd prefer a turkey, of course,' said Mr Thole, 'but times are hard.'

A PERFECTLY acceptable Watchnight Service followed. The singing was loud and lusty, if a little off-key at the back. The organist hit only a few dozen bum notes, instead of his usual waterfall of discord. Even the chink of carryout bottles at the back seemed not to offend too many people.

Mr Thole managed to tread a reasonably entertaining, spiritual and uplifting line with his sermon by conducting a question-and-answer session with his congregation.

'Do you know that if all the coins given over the course of a year at collections in this church were laid end to end,' he said, 'they would reach to Aberdeen and back seventeen times? Seventeen times. The people of the village and the vale should be proud of themselves for that.

'And do you know that if all the children's Bibles that we have helped to buy for schools in Africa were laid end to end, they would reach from Aberdeen to Edinburgh? We should be equally proud of that, don't you think?'

There was a small and genuine burst of applause at the back, which wafted forwards as even regular kirkgoers were prepared to risk a clap in their pews.

'And do you know,' continued Mr Thole, 'that if all the empty seats here on Sundays throughout the year were given to Pittodrie Stadium, the Dons could increase their crowd by half as much again?

There was a guilty silence for a moment, until Mr Thole continued: 'That is, if the Dons could find a crowd.'

There was a buzz of laughter, again starting at the back, and Mr

Thole felt his heart become a little lighter. It stayed lighter for all of two seconds, until his gaze fell upon Ebenezer Grip, third row back, second in from the left.

Ebenezer's face was devoid of any emotion. He looked as if he was on the point of a scowl , and then, when Ebenezer looked at his watch, Mr Thole felt his spirits begin to slide again.

IT was twenty minutes later, as the congregation was drifting away, anxious to be home before Santa did his rounds, that Mr Thole turned for the umpteenth time back towards the kirk door, hand outstretched, and found himself facing Ebenezer, who was pulling his coat about him.

'Mr Grip,' said Mr Thole, 'how very good of you to come out on such a sharp night.'

'I aye come, meenister, ye ken that. It wid tak mair nor a pickie frost tae pit me aff. Interestin service, by the by.'

'Did you think so?'

'Hinna heard een like that afore.'

Mr Thole was not sure if that was good or bad. 'Well,' he said, 'I thought I'd try something a little different.'

'Aa that layin end tae end stuff.'

'Yes, I thought it might send people home thinking.'

'It fairly sent Erchie Sotter hame thinkin.'

'Did it really? I do hope so. How do you know?'

'I heard him sayin as he met in wi Sandy Brose: 'If aa the fowk that wis sleepin in the kirk wis laid end tae end, they'd be a lot mair comfy.'

50 *Dorothy at the Doctor*

THE doctor looked at the next file on his desk and could feel his heart beginning to sink. He plodded towards the door of his consulting room, trying hard not to slouch into his gloom, and called towards the waiting room: 'Dorothy Birze, please.'

'Hello, ye,' came a cheery voice at his side, and he stepped away with a start then studied Dorothy as she peered up at him through her jamjar specs. 'I kent I wis next,' she said, 'so I jist thocht I'd stan aside yer door and save ye some time. I ken foo busy you doctors is nooadays. Will I awa in?'

The doctor took another step back and his enthusiastic patient trotted past. Before he could close the door behind him and sit at his desk, he found that Dorothy was up on the couch already, still wearing her tweed coat and teacosy hat, still clutching her handbag and now staring at the ceiling.

'Will I tak aff ma claes?' she said.

'No, that won't be necessary, not just yet,' the doctor said. 'I'd better be hearing about what seems to be the trouble first.'

'Ach, I'm affa doon the dumps,' Dorothy said. 'I dinna ken fit's adee. It cam ower me last wikkend, seein aa the femlies oot strollin in the fine weather, playin fitba in the pleasure park, haein their picnics.'

'And you felt as if you had nobody at all. You felt left out. You felt as if you had nothing to look forward to. You felt as if life was passing you by.'

There was a silence for a moment as Dorothy stared at the ceiling. 'Weel,' she said, 'if I wisna doon in the dumps afore, I'm certainly doon in the dumps noo. Congratulations.'

'I'm terribly sorry,' the doctor said. 'Was that not what you were going to tell me?'

Dorothy sighed and harumphed and squirmed a little on the coach, then turned her head to look at the doctor. 'I suppose it wis,' she said. 'It's jist a shock fin ye hear it said oot loud like that.'

'So you're maybe a little depressed, do you think? Are you very sleepy all the time? Can't be bothered with anything? Irritable? Eating for comfort, perhaps?'

Dorothy turned back to stare at the ceiling. The doctor saw that she was clutching her handbag a little more tightly. She began nodding. A hint of a tear began trickling down.

'It's all right,' he said. 'It's nothing to be embarrassed about. It's just a temporary chemical imbalance that you have, that's all. We can get you right as rain in no time.'

'I'm nae haein nae peels,' Dorothy said in a small, squeaky voice.

'It's perfectly all right. They're very mild. They're not addictive. They'll pick you up and settle you down and you'll soon be good as gold and we'll be able to get you off them as soon as you like.'

'Fit's their side effects?'

'Well, nothing really. One or two people susceptible to allergies report a slight rash, but we just switch them to another type. And, um, until we establish the correct daily dose by a process of trial and error, they might also depress the libido.'

Dorothy wiped away the tear and looked round. 'The fit?'

'The libido. The sex drive.'

'Och, I hinna been at een o them since 1959.' She smiled as the memory began washing over her. 'What a nicht that wis. There wis aboot eichty o's stappit intae the hall at Methlick. Ye hinna seen a nicht like it. Fowk pilin in aawye. Caicklin and lachin. Hardly room tae move. Squeezin ower een anither aa roon the place. I sweir some fowk hid tae dee't in the kitchen. It couldna hiv been hygienic, fit wi the bradies laid oot and aathing, bit that's the truth.

'We did it for the money, of coorse. We werena supposed til bit, ach, a bit hard cash spiced up things. Swappin partners. Drink. Raffles and a plate o stovies at half time. Aa for two and six. Ye dinna get value on a nicht oot like that nooadays. I aye felt sorry for the hallkeeper. What a sotter he must hiv hid tae redd up the next day. Isn't it funny, ye nivver hear o them noo?'

'Never hear of what?'

'Whist drives.'

'Not whist drives. Sex drives.'

'Oh, we nivver did nothing like that. Nae at Methlick.' She looked round at him again. 'What a fool thing tae say.' Then she beamed.

'There's a bit o the nickum in you, I'm thinkin, ye great big coorse loon. Fit are ye efter?'

'I'm after getting you sorted out.'

'Oh, you doctors is aa the same, ye silver-tongued devil.'

'I mean your illness. One of the side effects of the medication for some people is a reported loss of the sex drive.'

Dorothy looked at him again. 'Doctor,' she said. 'I'm near sivventy. Supposin ma man wis still alive, I dinna think the loss o ma li-lo wid bother me.'

'Libido.'

'That an aa. Tae be honest wi ye, doctor, I nivver could be deein wi that side o mairriage. I preferred ma knittin.'

'But I thought you had children.'

'I'd twa kids, ye're richt. Jist because I wisna muckle o a haun at the doon-belows didna mean ma man wis the same.' She clutched her handbag again. 'I think ye could safely say he wis quite demandin in that department.'

'Really? Well, perhaps that's why you didn't much care for the physical side of the relationship.'

'Three times a nicht on a Sunday and Monday. Twice a nicht on Tuesdays and Wednesdays. Once a nicht on Fridays and Setterdays.'

'What about Thursdays?'

'That wis the nicht he bade at hame wi me.'